'This book on the bullying of gay, lesbian  organised, sensible and packed with useful well as parents and pupils themselves. It c as a handbook to help tackle this important issue in the school context.'

– *Peter K. Smith, Goldsmiths, University of London, UK*

'As someone who has spent a lifetime dealing with the consequences of crime, harassment, bullying and hate in its various guises it is good to see this very practical articulation of how a whole-school approach to tackle homophobic bullying can intervene early to help prevent harm and contribute towards a society that is fair, just and inclusive. Prejudices, intolerance and fears are often set during childhood and that is why Avon and Somerset Constabulary has done its best to protect, indeed grow, our ability to work with and engage with schools. In the sensitive area of homophobic bullying, many will lack confidence and experience of how to respond. Jonathan has been offering advice to constabularies for many years and this book helps extend this to many more readers looking for insight and help.'

– *Andy Marsh QPM, Chief Constable, Avon and Somerset Constabulary*

'This is an essential read for any school leader who is serious about challenging homophobic and biphobic bullying – and that should be all school leaders! It provides straightforward, practical advice and will make sure you are meeting your legal and moral obligations to keep children safe.'

– *Lauren Seager-Smith FRSA, CEO Kidscape*

'Jonathan Charlesworth is the author of *That's So Gay!* and all his readers will welcome this new book. With his many years of experience – both in teaching and leading a charity challenging this form of bullying and discrimination – Jonathan Charlesworth brings a calm wisdom to an issue that schools, colleges and alternative provision often struggle to address successfully. Prejudice-related behaviour among students often reflects the environment our young people grow up in. This makes challenging prejudice and discrimination difficult when it may be learned at home or from the media and young people think it is justified. Schools will be better able to do so and make school a safe place with this book at their side.'

From the basics through to thoughtful considerations of complex situations, the author provides the essentials every teacher needs and will be inspired by. Charlesworth consulted young people and teachers and describes a gap between the lived experience of the young people and the views of the staff. These valuable insights should encourage schools to listen to their student body and change their interventions.

Recent changes in legislation in the UK and in Ireland, and a new curriculum for RSE, all have to be assimilated into practice along with the Equality Act. But this is no dry text about law. Threaded throughout are practical tips and advice for the sensitive handling of disclosures and practice strategies that schools will implement in modern Britain. This should be required reading in teacher training and for all pastoral leads. It will be essential for anyone handling behaviour in schools and a valuable complement to curricular work related to statutory RSE.'

– Adrienne Katz FRSA, Director of Youthworks and 2018
joint winner of Inspirational Individual of the Year
by the Ben Cohen StandUp Foundation

'School leaders often talk about moral purpose and creating a fair and just society. Jonathan Charlesworth continues to give direction, insight and practical guidance on matters very directly connected to this important aspect of what schools are about. Jonathan's expert exploration of key equalities issues inspired me – instilling confidence and understanding. School leaders seeking knowledge, insight and the assurance to recognise, stop and prevent homophobic or biphobic bullying will find it in this indispensable book.'

– Roland Lovatt, Headteacher, Yeo Moor Primary School,
Clevedon, North Somerset

'Education is about more than just the taught subjects on the school timetable. For an education to mean anything at all, our young people need to leave school with a sense of who they are. Our schools need to provide them with the skills, knowledge, character and confidence to assert their identity, in whatever form they find it. Bullying of any kind undermines that process so it is our responsibility as educators to challenge it. Jonathan Charlesworth offers an essential guide for educators who seek to understand the complexity of issues faced by young people concerning their emerging sexual identity. He explains accessibly the homophobic or biphobic bullying which can accompany the coming out (or indeed not coming out) of our lesbian, gay, bisexual or questioning students. If our schools are to be truly inclusive we must understand and adjust to enable all our young people to thrive – however they identify. Jonathan's book is a key part of our toolkit in developing the schools that all our children need.'

– Chris Hildrew, Headteacher, Churchill Academy &
Sixth Form, North Somerset

'We have worked with Jonathan and EACH several times and our students and staff have always gained so much from their time with him. His original book, which helped develop understanding of how to recognise, stop and prevent homophobic bullying, was vital to our key staff in this important and ever-evolving area. Jonathan's ability to allow informative, open discussion and debate in a safe and secure environment has really enabled all students to feel more equipped and empowered to deal with challenging topics. His experience and expertise are captured in this new book. We very much look forward to making best use of this.'

– Cameron Shaw, Principal, Bristol Metropolitan Academy

'We have been incredibly fortunate to have benefitted from Jonathan's outstanding work with our school over the last 10 years. He has helped us shape our school's attitudes and ethos regarding LGBT matters. He has delivered inspirational training to our staff that has engaged and educated, as well as being a key focus for developing our policy and practice across the LGBT field and homophobic and biphobic bullying. Further, and most importantly, Jonathan has had a huge impact on our student community: being thought provoking and challenging, yet balancing that with real sensitivity and an impressive ability to listen and empathise. We are proud to be associated with Jonathan's book, his work with EACH and he continues to be our "go-to" for his expert advice and guidance across this area of our students' lives and experiences.'

– Steve Moir, Headteacher at Bradley Stoke Community School,
South Gloucestershire

How to Stop Homophobic and Biphobic Bullying

of related interest

How to Transform Your School into an LGBT+ Friendly Place
A Practical Guide for Nursery, Primary and Secondary Teachers
Dr Elly Barnes MBE and Dr Anna Carlile
ISBN 978 1 78592 349 4
eISBN 978 1 78450 684 1

The Teacher's Guide to Resolving School Bullying
Evidence-Based Strategies and Pupil-Led Interventions
Elizabeth Nassem
ISBN 978 1 78592 419 4
eISBN 978 1 78450 785 5

Gender Equality in Primary Schools
A Guide for Teachers
Helen Griffin
ISBN 978 1 78592 340 1
eISBN 978 1 78450 661 2

How to Stop Homophobic and Biphobic Bullying

A PRACTICAL WHOLE-SCHOOL APPROACH

Jonathan Charlesworth M.Ed.

Foreword by Peter K. Smith

Jessica Kingsley Publishers
London and Philadelphia

First published in Great Britain in 2020 by Jessica Kingsley Publishers

An Hachette Company

1

Copyright © Jonathan Charlesworth 2020
Foreword copyright © Peter K. Smith 2020

Front cover image source: Shutterstock®.

A CIP catalogue record for this title is available from the British Library and the Library of Congress

ISBN 978 1 78775 306 8
eISBN 978 1 78775 307 5

Printed and bound in Great Britain by Clays

Jessica Kingsley Publishers' policy is to use papers that are natural, renewable and recyclable products and made from wood grown in sustainable forests. The logging and manufacturing processes are expected to conform to the environmental regulations of the country of origin.

Jessica Kingsley Publishers
73 Collier Street
London N1 9BE, UK

www.jkp.com

This book is dedicated to Adrian Andrews (1950–2017).
Sadly missed. Remembered daily.

Contents

Foreword

Unfortunately, homophobic and biphobic bullying are prevalent in schools in the UK and internationally. A vital part of education is to confront prejudiced views and behaviours whether about sexual orientation or identity, ethnicity, faith, gender, or disability – such as are manifested in prejudice-based or bias bullying. Schools should be a safe place for learning. In addition they should be imparting the values of tolerance of difference and helping others, as part of being a good citizen in later life.

Fortunately, this book by Jonathan Charlesworth will be an invaluable asset, so far as homophobic and biphobic bullying is concerned. When I read it I was impressed by the careful and balanced way it is written and the very systematic way in which he presents material. He naturally starts with a thorough description of what these kinds of bullying entail, who gets involved and some of the reasons why it can happen. He then describes the impact of being a target of such behaviours. We know from extensive research that targets of school bullying can experience anxiety, depression, feelings of loss of self-worth and even suicidal thoughts and behaviours. This is not inevitably so. It depends on how long and severe the bullying is, and some pupils have more support from friends or family, or more inner reserves of strength, and can come through relatively unscathed. But for the majority of targets there are adverse effects from mild to moderate to very severe: sometimes lasting into adult life. These are educational and health issues that cannot be ignored.

Dealing with homophobic and biphobic attitudes, and bullying behaviours, is one important part of this broad challenge. The second part of this book gives comprehensive help and advice for teachers, parents and others faced with these issues. This includes ways of supporting targets, ways of working to change those who are doing the bullying and broader issues around school policies and government requirements and guidelines. Homophobic and biphobic bullying can raise sensitive issues and bring up a range of attitudes about how best to deal with it. The author is aware of this, and writes sensibly and with consideration, without shirking the need to act firmly and decisively when the situation requires it. I would recommend this book as an excellent and authoritative guide: a book which hopefully every school will purchase, and use, as a support in how they work around these issues and with pupils involved in these kinds of behaviours.

Peter K. Smith
Goldsmiths, University of London
March 2020

Acknowledgements

I should like to thank the children, young people, parents and those with a professional responsibility for children with whom I have worked since 1985 and especially on the Department for Education initiatives *Safe to Learn, Inspiring Equality in Education, Learn Equality, Live Equal* and the National Lottery funded five-year programme Reach. I am particularly grateful to the pupils and teachers of Churchill Academy and Sixth Form, Gordano School, Backwell School, St John the Evangelist Primary School and Yeo Moor Primary School in North Somerset; Bradley Stoke Community School, Sir Bernard Lovell Academy, Almondsbury Primary School and Horton Primary School in South Gloucestershire; Bristol Brunel Academy, Bristol Metropolitan Academy, Cotham School, St Mary Redcliffe School, Elmlea Junior School, Ashley Down Primary School and Little Mead Primary Academy in Bristol; Wyedean School and Sixth Form Centre in Gloucestershire; Talbot Heath School in Dorset and Corsham School in Wiltshire.

Although essentially for those with concerns about homophobic or biphobic bullying, and eager to find ways to recognise, stop and prevent it, this book may also be valuable to anyone coming to understand their own sexual orientation or that of someone about whom they care.

I have been hugely inspired by the many words of wisdom emanating from children and young people about the ways we can all work together to challenge homophobic and biphobic bullying in our schools.

My sincere thanks go to Jahna Hampshire, my Editorial Assistant, whose insights and contributions to this book have been invaluable.

Preface

This book is an explanation of and a practical guide to challenging homophobic or biphobic language, name-calling and bullying. I have used variously the words, lesbian, gay and bisexual throughout the book. Unless I am making a specific point about, say, bisexuality, any use of the three applies equally to the other two and homophobia includes biphobia and lesbophobia.

Although homophobia and transphobia can 'look' alike, the issues of sexuality and gender identity are discrete. There is often a case for viewing the issues pertinent to lesbian, gay, bisexual and transgender people collectively but homophobic bullying and transphobic bullying 'come from' different places. Challenging transphobic bullying warrants its own focus in a dedicated book and this is why it is not included in *How to Stop Homophobic and Biphobic Bullying*. At the end of this book, you will find signposting to resources which should help you address transphobic bullying.

Throughout the book, 'parents' includes grandparents, carers and guardians. 'Pupils' includes learners and students. 'Governors' includes trustees. 'Sexuality' and 'sexual orientation' are used interchangeably. The named audience throughout this book is schools but if you are a college tutor, youth worker, university lecturer, or someone who works in any children's service, the messages are equally applicable to your own work and young people.

Introduction

Since the first edition of this book in 2015 we have seen the introduction of new Relationships and Sex Education (RSE) in England in September 2019, which is mandatory in all schools from September 2020, the drafting of new Relationships and Sexuality Education which will come into effect in Wales in 2020 and the Welsh Government's publication of *Rights, Respect, Equality: Guidance for Schools: Statutory Anti-Bullying Guidance* to all its schools in November 2019. The Department for Education (2017c) launched its *Preventing and Tackling Bullying* guidance in July 2017 and the 2019 Ofsted framework furthers its commitment to treating pupil wellbeing as a measure of success, citing the prevention of bullying (including homophobic and biphobic bullying) and effective provision of RSE and personal, social and health education (PSHE) as key measurements.

In 2017, Turing's law posthumously pardoned thousands of gay men convicted of offences that criminalised same-sex activity (Bowcott, 2017). 2019 saw the introduction of equal marriage rights in Northern Ireland. Lesbian, gay and bisexual people have more representation in mainstream media. Reports of anti-gay and lesbian hate crimes however, doubled in the five years between 2014 and 2019 (Marsh, Mohdin and McIntyre, 2019). Gay conversion therapy is still legal in the UK, and schools teaching about families with lesbian, gay or bisexual parents face protests (Ashenden and Parsons, 2019). Seventy per cent of lesbian, gay, bisexual and transgender (LGBT) people have been sexually harassed at work (Trade Union Congress, 2019), while public acceptance of gay sex is falling for the first time since the AIDS crisis (Booth, 2019).

These society-wide issues affect our pupils, contributing to homophobic bullying being the most common form of bullying in schools (BBC, 2019). Seventy-one per cent of teachers report witnessing homophobic bullying and 31 per cent report witnessing it at least once a month (Sky News, 2019).

Although one would think schools would be places where one would see lots of discussion and 'ground breaking' when it comes to equalities issues they are actually largely conservative places that are invariably behind change, seldom ahead of it. This is why issues of sexuality rarely get discussed except when raised by forward-looking teachers who usually have a personal connection with the issue which has brought it into their consciousness or there is a problem with which to be dealt.

Since 1999, UK society has witnessed landslide and welcome legislative changes advancing equalities rights and creating a more equal workplace for people who are gay. Legal improvements have increased gay people's sense of belonging to 'mainstream' society rather than feeling, as they have for too long, invisible, excluded and often ostracised from it.

We have seen this change reflected in media, television, film and advertising. One of the results of this is that gay young people are more confident about 'coming out' (acknowledging being gay, lesbian or bisexual) while pupils at school rather than waiting until they are in the workplace or at college or university.

> Parents don't know if their child is heterosexual so it contradicts the argument that children are too young to attend the LGBT group. (Daisy, 13)

We should recognise that pupils are exploring their sexuality at a younger age than at any time in modern history (facilitated by sexting and online pornography consumption) and that lesbian, gay and bisexual young people are accordingly coming out at a younger age – affirmed as they are by positive role models such as Amandla Stenberg, Ellen Page, Frank Ocean, Jim Parsons, Adele Roberts, Jacqueline Wilson and Olly Alexander, and changes in legislation which they see around them.

Although coming out is happening sooner it remains problematic for many school-age people to 'be cool' about a friend or peer being gay. I have lost count of the number of teachers who have reassured me 'but Jason has heaps of friends!' – who all turn out to be girls. What this means is that Jason does not benefit from a balance of friends (by gender). He is coping strategically with a problem. He is not thriving and integrated, even if at the time he and his teachers fail to recognise this.

A dichotomy exists between the lesbian, gay or bisexual individuals and characters heterosexual young people enjoy watching on television

– Alan Carr, Sue Perkins, Graham Norton, RuPaul, Ruby Rose, Kevin and Cheryl from *Riverdale* – and having that reality in their classroom or actually at home in their living room or bedroom. Young people often like to give the impression they know everything they need to know and what they do not know is dull, boring or uninteresting – often described as gay. Many young people however experience the wider world in the main through handheld devices, desktop PCs and television and the pupils interviewed for this book cited over and over how incredulous their peers were when as an individual they came out as lesbian, gay or bisexual.

This dichotomy set up by media portrayals of lesbian or bisexual identities can be particularly palpable for girls. There is an increasing concern about the impact of the media on young women and the way their lives continue to be constrained by sexual harassment: workplace discrimination, street harassment and body-shaming. All girls will be attempting to navigate the fine line set out in films, music, magazines and blogs for them to be sexy but not sexual (Tolman, 2009). This contradiction is especially evident for lesbians whose personalities are either conflated with pornography or dismissed as frigid. For a girl to come out as a lesbian or bisexual is in many ways to commit a 'double violation' as she is expressing sexual attraction and it is for the same gender (Tolman, 2009, p.185). Girls and young women who come out as lesbian or bisexual are often faced with incredulity or a heightened level of sexual interest or harassment.

I came out as bisexual in Year 7; at the time I didn't know the word for it. Now I know I'm not weird – there is a word for it. (Daisy, 13)

It is not at all uncommon today for young people to come out at 13 or 14 years of age, or younger. This does not mean that individuals are not fearful of the ramifications. Harassment and homophobic bullying remain a distinct possibility for too many lesbian, gay and bisexual young people. The younger one's peers are when someone comes out the less is their emotional maturity to accept the revelation and adapt to the perceived 'difference' in the friend 'they thought they knew'. Added to this is the potential for ostracism from parents and other loved ones. Rejection by peers is bad enough but that by one's own parents is the most painful of all.

Each pupil attending school has the right to an education which fires the imagination and promotes the realisation of every aspect of potential available to that young person during their time there. Teachers are essentially very effective gatekeepers to this education, exerting huge power to either facilitate or block it. It is however their legal and moral duty to promote it to the best of their abilities.

Lesbian, gay and bisexual pupils deserve to be treated with the same respect as their heterosexual peers while at school and in anticipation of their role within adult society. Teachers have a duty of care to nurture and develop values such as empathy, understanding and respect for every pupil and towards every pupil. Teachers can help change the culture in their own classroom while headteachers can bring about whole-school change by 'leading from the front' with confidence and conviction. Straightforward practice such as the use of appropriate language, what is placed on noticeboards (or not), on websites (or not) or the choice of outside speakers sends powerful messages about what is valued, endorsed or matters.

CASE STUDY: Bristol Metropolitan Academy

The Old Vic came and ran a weekly after-school drama workshop with our Year 7s/8s during the course of a year. Their brief was to write their own play and our students chose to make the focus of their production 'human rights and respecting others'. As part of their production, students wore Pride flags and one of the lines was that a student was asked to 'Stand straight' and she commented back 'But I'm gay!' This was then presented at the Old Vic in April as a medley of performances from other schools across Bristol and families of students were invited.

Nicola Hooper, Head of House, Bristol Metropolitan Academy, Bristol

Too often in schools we talk about LGBT issues in terms of homophobic bullying and not in terms of 'normalising' the topic by discussing rights, respect, equality, history and justice. In the UK, this is without doubt one of the legacies of Section 28 of the Local Government Act 1988: effectively choking off constructive discussion between teachers and pupils, pupils and pupils and teachers and teachers for 15 years (see Appendix 1). But the cast of Section 28's shadow did not stop in 2003 in the year of its repeal. My teaching, training and consultancy to and for schools since 1985 has reflected time after time how unconfident teachers are, on a number of levels, to address matters of sexual orientation. It has come down to a brave sole teacher to pick up the issue either because they have someone in their personal life who is lesbian, gay or bisexual or they are attempting to support a pupil and so often need to reach out for support beyond the school gates and seek support from Educational Action Challenging Homophobia (EACH) or another service provider.

Bullying will continue until adults cease to model it to children so very effectively and so regularly: during Prime Minister's Questions in the House of Commons, in reality TV shows and within sports fixtures. Children simply copy what they see adults doing – this is part of what 'growing up' means to them. The wellbeing of pupils in our schools is paramount and part of teachers' responsibilities. Schools who fail to adequately safeguard this (including protecting young people from bullying and harassment) are failing to meet their responsibilities both in law and their duty of care.

Homophobic bullying is never just 'banter', a 'joke' or 'a bit of a drama'. It can cause major fear and trauma, increase the likelihood of various forms of self-harm and seriously limit aspirations and achievement. The effects of exposure to bullying can lead well into adulthood: ruining individuals' lives.

We all have the power however to do something to challenge bullying – including homophobic and biphobic bullying – and I trust you will find this book a practical one to help you and your school, college or other youth setting to better understand what is homophobic or biphobic bullying, who experiences it (and why), its impact and what you should and can do about it (and why). It will also guide you towards creating an inclusive school which prevents all forms of bullying and challenges name-calling. When children are being bullied, the achievement of all or any of the government's desired outcomes will be seriously undermined.

Along the way, you will learn how to work with those who bully homophobically or biphobically. Since 2000 when I started working full-time to challenge homophobic bullying and harassment, 'gay' has been the word which remains for far too many children and young adults the one of choice to put down, insult, 'diss' or cuss someone when actually it is an adjective to describe a sexual orientation or a word found in poetry, prose and music to describe brightness, jollity and cheerfulness. Our failure as adults to challenge 'gay' when used offensively (either deliberately or inadvertently) readily paves the way for homophobic and biphobic bullying. So let us begin by acknowledging in every classroom that in society some people are lesbian, gay or bisexual. They have protection in law and are entitled to respect. So let's talk about it.

CHAPTER 1

What Is Homophobic and Biphobic Bullying?

Bullying is behaviour by an individual or a group which is usually repeated over time. Its purpose is to intentionally hurt either another individual or group emotionally and sometimes physically.

Homophobic and biphobic bullying happens in both primary and secondary schools and in a variety of ways. It is a specific form of bullying motivated by prejudice against lesbian, gay and bisexual people, those perceived to be gay, someone with a lesbian, gay or bisexual relative or simply because the target is different in some way. When aimed at those identified by the perpetrator as 'different' this can be because the target does not conform to 'expected' or 'gender appropriate' behaviour. It is the person's identity which is used to abuse them and homophobic or biphobic bullying can therefore be experienced by a young person regardless of their sexuality.

At its most benign, it is voiced as a passive dislike of lesbian, gay or bisexual people. At its most destructive it involves active victimisation. Homophobic and biphobic bullying is not characterised by specific acts but by the negative attitudes and beliefs towards lesbian, gay and bisexual people which underlie these acts. If homophobic and biphobic bullying, or any form of prejudice-based bullying, is addressed solely as an issue of discipline the underlying causes will remain unchallenged.

Like all bullying, homophobic and biphobic bullying can present itself in different forms, both direct and indirect. Table 1.1 comprehensively details the different ways in which bullying can be experienced (London Borough of Wandsworth Safeguarding Children Board, 2012). Direct forms of bullying include name-calling, offensive messages or tweets, comparing pupils to stereotyped gay, bisexual or lesbian caricatures and, too often, violent physical assaults. Indirect forms of bullying may include rumour-mongering, being left out or vandalism. This abuse can take place in corridors, classrooms, playgrounds, at youth centres or after-school clubs and even in the privacy of one's home via the internet.

Homophobic language is frequently used without its perpetrators thinking and is often ignored because it can be difficult to know how to respond without awareness and appropriate training. It is regularly brushed off as 'harmless banter' and not thought to be particularly hurtful. Such language and attitudes in schools need to be challenged, however, because ignoring them allows homophobic and biphobic bullying to gain a foothold, continue and then escalate.

Homophobic language and abuse starts in primary school where pupils may call each other, or indeed inanimate objects, 'gay' without really understanding what this means. If such use is not challenged at this stage it will appear acceptable, making it more difficult to address in secondary school. Children may also experience verbal bullying because they have a lesbian, gay or bisexual parent or sibling. It is very common for a primary school to first 'meet' homophobic bullying when one of its pupils has 'two mums'.

Pupils can also experience indirect homophobic or biphobic abuse not directed towards a particular person or group but when remarks are made to pass negative judgement, such as 'rounders is gay' or 'your ringtone is so gay'. It is important for all staff to challenge pupils and explain the consequences of using 'gay' in a derogatory way. It might be time consuming at first but a consistent approach in challenging such language is vital to achieving progress and the creation of an environment in which being lesbian, gay or bisexual is not thought of in negative terms.

> I don't hear homophobic comments around the school and I'm alert to this as I'm a gay man. Also, the pupils will and do challenge each other over homophobic language and name-calling, saying 'That's inappropriate' when it arises. I'd urge any pupil to tell their teacher at the end of their lesson (or when opportune) that they've heard or suffered homophobic name-calling. (Secondary school teacher)

Direct homophobic or biphobic abuse can be directed towards an individual or group of pupils as a one-off incident or repeatedly. A boy who is called 'poof' or hears 'faggot' when he walks by, or a girl who is called a 'dyke' or a 'lezzer' and avoided as she walks along the school corridor, or a pupil considered to be or out as bisexual called a 'greedy slag' outside the school gates can suffer both short- and long-term harm.

In secondary school, homophobic language might be extensive and used directly or indirectly to:

- ridicule or denigrate something considered inferior or risible – 'Circle Time is so gay!'

- harass a pupil with a gay parent, sibling or in-law – 'Your dad left you 'cos he's a gay boy!'

- disparage the actions of another – 'You play the flute? That is well gay!'

- imply that a response to a call to action is unacceptable – 'It's a show I'd have to sing in? That's too gay!'

- intimidate someone or make them feel uncomfortable – 'Sir, do you like musicals?' or 'Miss, do you have cats?'

- undermine and bully someone by suggesting that they are a lesbian, including spreading rumours and malicious gossip – 'Samira's so hairy! She gotta be a lesbian!'

- verbally bully someone who is bisexual, or who is thought to be – 'Have some more cake bi-boy! Greedy by name greedy by nature!'

Homophobic and biphobic bullying increasingly take place through cyberbullying, i.e. phone calls, text messaging, picture/video messaging, email and via various social media platforms. Through modern technology, vicious comments can be made and rumours spread about a person's sexual orientation. Whole communities become bystanders as these incidents largely go unreported. Advances in technology have transformed the bullying landscape with new tools such as smartphones and mobile phone applications providing platforms to target pupils directly or indirectly 24 hours a day, seven days a week. This can make it harder for educators and parents to recognise when it is going on. Schools need to ensure that they are alert to the risks of cyberbullying and include provision for it within their anti-bullying policies.

TABLE 1.1: THE WAYS IN WHICH BULLYING CAN BE EXPERIENCED

BEHAVIOUR	PERSONAL ASPECTS	SOCIAL ASPECTS	CRIMINAL
Verbal bullying that is deliberately intended to hurt, intimidate, frighten, harm or exclude	• Name-calling, belittling comments, jokes or verbal attacks based on appearance, home situation, sexuality, family • Nasty teasing hurting a person's feelings • Sexual harassment • Making personal threats	• Alienating a person from their friends and social groups • Damaging a reputation • Excluding and not including in small or larger group activities • Spreading rumours • Using sexually abusive or suggestive language to exclude a person or group • Ostracising • Malicious gossiping	• Coercing people or daring them to do illegal acts • Inciting others to do dangerous things • Inciting hatred towards an individual or group • Homophobic harassment • Threats about damaging a person, their family, friends or property, including inflicting physical harm • Intimidating telephone calls • Homophobic taunting
Non-verbal bullying that is deliberately intended to hurt, intimidate, harm, exclude or frighten	• Intimidation through gesture • Hiding, stealing or damaging a person's books or belongings • Dirty looks • Sending written threats	• Setting someone up to take the blame publicly • Shunning someone – not speaking with or interacting with them • 'Kissing teeth' (to express disapproval by clicking one's tongue behind one's teeth)	• Theft • Stalking

Physical bullying includes: a direct physical attack on a person or an indirect attack on property or belongings	• Beating • Biting • Choking • Kicking • Punching • Shaking • Slapping • Tripping • Spitting • Hitting • Poking • Throwing • Shoving • Urinating • Groping or unwanted touching • Ignoring	• Embarrassment and public humiliation • Group bullying – when a child or young person is outnumbered or picked on in some of the following ways: blocking the way, demanding money, being forced to participate in embarrassing initiation rites, being forced to do unwanted things in front of others, having belongings destroyed, stolen and/or ridiculed	• Extortion with threats • Sexual abuse • Sexual violence • Threatening with a weapon • Using a weapon to inflict harm • Physical assault • Stealing • 'Happy slapping' • Criminal damage
Cyberbullying: the majority of verbal and non-verbal behaviours can be carried out using new forms of technology – therefore cyberbullying takes the same form as non-physical victimisation, but without the bully having to confront the victim face to face; it is often carried out anonymously	• Sending threatening or intimidating comments via email, text messages, social media • Making malicious or prank phone calls • Instant messaging • Internet chat rooms • Personal websites • Creating web pages which aim to intimidate psychologically and/or physically threaten, or socially damage an individual or group	• Taking embarrassing or humiliating pictures or video clips on mobile phones which may also be sent or shared with others • Setting up or contributing to online forums or websites, where users post malicious comments about a person or group (e.g. trolling)	• Using any of these technological methods to threaten, intimidate or harass an individual or group

Box 1.1: Youthworks Cybersurvey

The Youthworks Cybersurvey surveyed young people in Suffolk to gain a greater understanding of how they use the internet. Responses from 1961 young people were collected in the autumn term of 2017 from 26 different schools and respondents were aged between 10 and 16 years old.

- Young people are spending increasing amounts of time online – with 19 per cent spending more than five hours online every day.

- Twenty-two per cent said they had been the target of cyberbullying.

- Twelve per cent of young people reported being threatened or their family being threatened online.

- Twelve per cent had met up with someone they only knew online.

- In 2019, 15 per cent of young people nationally aged 11–16 received messages containing insults about LGBT people (Youthworks, personal communication, 2019)

(Youthworks, 2017 and 2019)

Verbal abuse

Broadly speaking, the use of homophobic language and verbal abuse is the most common form of homophobic and biphobic harassment in schools. This includes name-calling, teasing and threatening another person because of their sexuality, perceived sexuality or association with people who are lesbian, gay or bisexual.

It is cited that the use of phrases such as 'That's so gay' to deem something as rubbish or inferior is 'endemic' within UK schools. One activity EACH delivers during workshops with pupils explores common insults heard throughout a typical school day and identifies which aspect of a person's identity these insults are targeting (see Box 1.2). Invariably pupils cite the regular use of language targeting someone's sexuality, weight, attractiveness, disability, race or gender.

When pupils start identifying these insults, the sheer number of derogatory labels that they associate with being lesbian, gay or bisexual never ceases to surprise. By contrast, if one tasks someone with thinking of a synonym for 'heterosexual' they will invariably only be able to come up with one: 'straight'. Homophobic language often includes derogatory words such as 'dyke', 'faggot' or 'queer' as well as phrases which reduce lesbian, gay or bisexual identities to sexual acts described in explicit or aggressive language. Of course, this language use varies depending on the setting and many pupils will be aware that it is unacceptable. As a result, they may be careful not to use it in the presence of teachers or other authority figures.

All the time I hear the boys saying 'you fag' or 'you're a tranny' to each other and its done out of the earshot of teachers. (Riley, 14)

When one engages pupils in an honest discussion about the abuse they hear it is clear this language sits within their everyday lexicon and needs to be challenged.

The people who notice it the most are the students. The teachers don't see it, because kids are clever. They know when and how to be rude and discriminatory and how to get away with it. They know who to target and who will allow them to get away with it. Bullies always learn how to work their way around things. They are very intricate. (Max, 16)

Box 1.2: Activity idea: Targeting differences

Divide your pupils into small groups and provide them with sticky notes. Give each group two minutes to list all the taunts and insults they regularly hear around school.

Once the pupils have listed these invite them to group them into aspects of 'difference'. This may include appearance, size, intelligence, skin colour, faith, sexuality, gender or physical impairment.

Once the pupils have identified these common groups ask the whole class to discuss:

- What aspect of 'difference' attract the most insults?

- In what situations are these insults used?

- What do these insults say about what is 'normal' and 'acceptable'?

- Where might messages of what is 'normal' and 'acceptable' come from?

Establish with pupils opportunities to challenge this use of language as an individual, as a class and as a school.

Adapted from EACH (2014)

While the use of 'gay' and 'That's so gay' to describe something as stupid, uncool, rubbish or boring is not as overtly abusive as some of the language cited above, it is no less problematic. It can be harder to challenge as it does not always accompany bullying. More often than not it is used in reference to situations or to describe objects rather than target an individual. As a result, pupils may not recognise that this language use is inappropriate and argue that calling their homework gay has nothing to do with their opinions on same-sex relationships. In fact, some pupils who identify as lesbian, gay or bisexual also use this language. What these pupils should recognise is that its use reinforces implicit prejudices and derogatory labels about lesbian, gay and bisexual people (broken, worthless, wrong) against which the gay rights movement has been campaigning for very many decades (see Box 1.3). Educators should recognise that phrases such as 'That's so gay' do not exist in isolation from the homophobic and biphobic abuse that is played out in wider society. A simple phrase going unchallenged can too often escalate into more overt abuse.

Box 1.3: Good As You

The term 'gay' is used to describe both men who are attracted to men and just as often today women who are attracted to women. There is wide agreement its use in this context emerged as part of the civil rights struggle of the 1960s and 1970s where, as an acronym, it spelt out 'Good As You' on marchers' banners. The banner at the time would have read 'Rights for homosexuals [sic]. We're as Good As You!'

Box 1.4: 'That's so gay' and homophobia

Jack – People around our school all the time say 'That's so gay!' but they just mean it as a negative, not directed at an individual. It's aimed at something like a game, not a person.

Lillian – It's still a bad thing to say.

Sarah – There are so many other words.

Lillian – Yeah! You're just reinforcing the idea that it's a bad idea to be gay.

Jack – Teachers must hear it because it goes round so much but they don't do anything about it.

Mika – If a comment is direct and bullying then a teacher would do something about it but otherwise they'd just let it go.

Lillian – They should challenge it!

Jenny – All teachers should challenge it consistently so a clear message is being given to everyone in the school.

Mika – If a teacher called out homophobic language in front of the class it would have an impact.

Lillian – The history of words needs to be explained and how fights for equality have been fought so concepts are placed in context.

Mika – I think if people had the history of these words explained they'd be more likely to stop because they're just told to stop without any explanation being given. No one understands why it's so bad to use.

Jack – People just throw around 'gay' like it's nothing. Even if it doesn't mean gay as in a person there's still that connection with gay being bad.

Secondary school pupils aged 14–16

Physical abuse

As the name suggests, physical bullying includes hitting, punching and kicking. This is arguably the most visible form of homophobic or biphobic bullying and more commonly reported among boys who are often both its targets and perpetrators. Despite this, we should be wary not to dismiss this behaviour as 'boys being boys' nor regard it as exceptional when girls engage in physical bullying or boys in ostracism.

When physical bullying does occur it can be a matter for the police. This is covered in Chapter 7. Physical abuse can include inappropriate touching or sexual assault. This is less likely to be recognised or reported.

Just as homophobic language can often reduce lesbian, gay or bisexual people to sex acts, inappropriate touching may include 'simulating' sex acts associated with being lesbian, gay or bisexual. It can also include pressuring a young person to 'prove' they are not lesbian or gay by kissing a girl or boy, allowing themselves to be touched or touching someone else sexually.

Indirect bullying

Indirect forms of bullying may involve stealing, damage to property, graffiti or intimidating looks. In some cases, this form of bullying can be extremely difficult to detect by those who are not the target. Relational bullying and cyberbullying are often (although not always) examples of indirect bullying.

> I get a lot of stares. There's this group of girls. They aren't very kind. Not up to bullying just not kind. (Lilah, 13)

Relational bullying

Relational bullying refers to rumour-mongering, ignoring or ostracising with the intention of damaging friendships or relationships. This form of bullying is less visible than explicit forms such as verbal and physical abuse but no less distressing.

> When I came out as a bisexual girl, everybody would move away from me. I lost some friends because of it. Some of my friends who were girls stopped hanging out with me. When I asked them why, they said they'd found some new friends. When I asked their friends, they told me it was because I'm bisexual and like girls and boys. (Cola, 13)

When pupils are ostracised, four fundamental needs, according to Maslow's hierarchy of needs (Maslow, 1943), are threatened:

- Belonging
- Self-esteem
- Control
- Meaningful existence.

This kind of bullying can be taking place face to face but it frequently manifests itself online. Pupils 'unfriending' someone on Facebook, unfollowing them on Instagram or Twitter or spreading rumours via social media are examples. Educators may not always recognise the very tangible impact that being ostracised online can have on a young person's relationships and friendships. All it takes is a click of a button for a rumour to 'go viral' reaching hundreds or even thousands. The impact of this on a young person's emotional wellbeing should never be underestimated.

Cyberbullying

Cyberbullying refers to the harassment of others through digital technologies such as mobile phones, computers, tablets or other devices with the intention of causing harm either directly or indirectly. This can include abusive messages via text or social media, web pages and groups set up specifically to spread hateful messages or rumours, silent and malicious calls, blackmailing and taking photos or videos and sharing these over the internet or mobile networks without consent. The casual use of homophobic or biphobic language online has also been highlighted by 'nohomophobes.com' (see Box 1.5).

Cyberbullying can have the following distinct features which set it apart from other forms of bullying:

- Impact: the scale and scope of cyberbullying can be greater than for other forms of bullying.

- Targets and perpetrators: the people involved may have a different profile to traditional bullies and their targets.

- Location: the 24/7 and 'anyplace' nature of cyberbullying is distinctive.

- Anonymity: the person being bullied will not always know who is attacking them.

- Motivation: some pupils may not be aware that what they are doing is bullying.

- Evidence: unlike other forms of bullying, the target of such bullying always has the evidence.

Box 1.5: Nohomophobes.com

Nohomophobes (Wells, 2019) is a website designed by the University of Alberta's Institute for Sexual Minority Studies and Services. It was established on 5 July 2012 to be a 'social mirror' reflecting the pervasiveness of casual homophobic language in society. The website achieves this by keeping an ongoing counter of how frequently the words 'faggot', 'dyke', 'no homo' and 'so gay' are used on Twitter. As of 2 December 2019:

- 41,116,413 uses of 'faggot'

- 7,919,163 uses of 'dyke'

- 15,378,544 uses of 'no homo'

- 13,538,048 uses of 'so gay'.

Why is homophobic and biphobic bullying the least reported form of bullying?

One of the key challenges EACH and other service providers face is that they know it goes on but homophobic and biphobic bullying is rarely reported. There are a number of reasons pupils cite as to why they do not report this type of bullying in school.

It is often felt that to report homophobic or biphobic bullying is to draw attention to one's sexuality. As a result, pupils who may be lesbian, gay or bisexual but not ready to come out will be reluctant to report bullying behaviour for fear of attracting further questioning. Similarly, pupils who are heterosexual can feel that reporting homophobic or biphobic bullying is akin to coming out as lesbian, gay or bisexual.

A lot of pupils may be reluctant to admit that they are upset by homophobic or biphobic abuse. The desire not to be seen as weak or a victim can make pupils reluctant to report any form of bullying. With homophobic and biphobic bullying, this can be more palpable as it is so often dismissed as 'banter', 'a drama' or 'just a joke' – therefore to report it would be seen to be taking it too seriously and attract further abuse. Finally, we know that pupils are unconfident in the mechanisms schools put in place to respond to bullying.

> Pupils don't tell in school because it normally just causes trouble.
> (Syd, 13)

Too many feel that their teachers will not take the problem seriously. They can also be unsure how to report if homophobic bullying is not specifically cited as unacceptable within school policies and practice. In addition, pupils often recognise a lack of clear and consistent sanctions in school when responding to bullying. Many fear that by reporting bullying they themselves will be excluded from activities in order to avoid being targeted by their perpetrator(s). EACH regularly hears stories of targeted pupils being asked to change separately for sports lessons and physical education or leave lessons early in order to avoid running into their tormentors.

Chapter 2 identifies common scenarios in which pupils experience homophobic and biphobic bullying. This will build on the understanding of what this bullying looks like and provide further insights as to why pupils may be reticent to report it. The next chapter also highlights how anyone can become a target regardless of sexual orientation.

KEY POINTS

✓ Homophobic and biphobic bullying is not necessarily characterised by specific acts but by the negative attitudes and beliefs towards lesbian, gay and bisexual people which underlie it.

✓ Relational bullying and cyberbullying can be less recognisable than verbal and physical bullying but equally damaging.

✓ Pupils are often unconfident that school mechanisms will effectively deal with bullying and fear reporting homophobic or biphobic bullying is akin to coming out.

✓ Casual homophobic language is pervasive offline and online and simple phrases such as 'That's so gay' left unchallenged can escalate into more overt abuse.

✓ Teachers need to actively engage pupils in discussions about homophobic and biphobic bullying to gain an accurate insight into pupils' attitudes and experiences of this prejudice-based bullying.

Who Experiences Homophobic and Biphobic Bullying?

It can often be assumed that homophobic or biphobic bullying only impacts upon lesbian, gay or bisexual pupils. The reality is that it affects all young people regardless of their sexual orientation. Many pupils will experience homophobic or biphobic bullying before they, or those perpetrating it, are even aware of their own sexual orientation. It is important therefore that we do not make assumptions about those involved.

Young people can hear of issues regarding sexuality from a number of sources. What they hear is often based on myth, misinformation or outright prejudice. By the time many young people begin to understand their sexuality the very labels lesbian, gay or bisexual have been stigmatised. With the world constantly promoting heterosexuality as the norm realising you are gay, lesbian or bisexual (or the assumption having been made that you are) can be a distressing experience. Stereotypes can cause young people to feel obliged to consciously or unconsciously prove that they are not gay. This curtails the freedom of expression and individuality of all young people.

Ultimately every young person will experience the limiting effects of homophobic and biphobic bullying be they the perpetrator, target or bystander. Challenging such bullying is for the benefit of everyone in your school. The values and attitudes that homophobia and biphobia reinforce make it difficult for young people to appreciate the diverse people who will soon become their college or university peers, work colleagues, family members and so on. If the role of school is to prepare young people for wider society it is failure on the part of us as educators to let these values and attitudes go unchallenged.

While the reasons young people experience homophobic bullying vary depending on their specific circumstances, common motives can nevertheless be identified. Understanding why some young people are targeted over others can help schools to identify the underlying beliefs that fuel this prejudice and to consider ways to challenge the attitudes of perpetrators. The sections below explore case studies in order to understand the different reasons young people experience homophobic and biphobic bullying.

Lesbian, gay or bisexual pupils

At age 13 I confided in my best friend that I was gay before I'd even understood myself what this meant. His brother outed me to the school and eventually I had to change schools because of the bullying. (Ralph, 21)

Young people who are lesbian, gay or bisexual are the most vulnerable to homophobic bullying. Even if they are not the direct targets witnessing it can cause negative messages and stereotypes about one's identity to become internalised. All too often young people only ever hear about lesbian, gay and bisexual young people being bullied, assaulted or abused because of their sexuality. Bullying and tragedy can be seen as inevitable for such young people. It is the responsibility of school staff to ensure that all pupils feel safe and understand that homophobic and biphobic bullying will not be tolerated. It is possible for gay young people to be resilient to and resist negative messages about their identity and in order to do this they require affirmative and accurate information about their lives.

I'm 16 and I know I'm a lesbian but I'm terrified to tell anyone in my family in case they stop loving me. My parents are divorced and my brother's always making really homophobic comments. I'm scared to tell any of my friends as no one I know is gay and I'm frightened I'd be rejected by them too. (Linda, 16)

Homophobic comments, even when not targeted directly at the individual, can make young people feel ostracised. As a result, individuals like Linda may feel they have to hide who they are so their family, friends or school community will accept them. In homophobic or biphobic environments many gay young people will deny their sexual orientation to themselves or others. All too often experiences such as Linda's can be ignored.

It is important you are aware that you may not always know who in your school is lesbian, gay or bisexual and we should not make assumptions about the sexual orientation of the people with whom we work. Lesbian, gay and bisexual people of all ages can find themselves emotionally exhausted by having to reconcile how they are feeling inside with the problems others have in understanding, recognising and accepting their sexuality.

Different stigmas are attached to the labels lesbian, gay and bisexual. Young people, and adults alike who are bisexual can face discrimination from their heterosexual, lesbian and gay peers. Being told to 'pick a side' is not an uncommon experience for bisexual people.

People want you to be one thing or the other. Bisexuality is seen as unacceptable: you're either one or the other. (Elsie, 13)

We can so often get called 'indecisive' as a bisexual person. (Britney, 14)

Many people see bisexuality as synonymous with promiscuity although this is not the case. The assumption that bisexual people are promiscuous can make them the target of sexual harassment and bullying. While some young people who identify as bisexual will go on to identify as heterosexual, lesbian or gay, many will not. All young people should have a right to come to this understanding of their sexual orientation free from abuse and harassment. It is common for the experiences of bisexual young people to be dismissed as 'just a phase'. As a result, their experience of bullying may be belittled or underestimated.

Lesbian, gay or bisexual by association

When my partner David and I moved to a new town for my job our son had to move primary school. Since then he has been the target of homophobic bullying from the majority of his peers. The other boys call him 'gay boy', exclude him from their games and tell him he has to hang out with the girls. We have reported it to the school but most of the bullying takes place on the playground so they barely notice it. He is only 11 but he has started to walk home from school by himself because he hates it when we come to pick him up. I'm concerned that the harassment will continue into secondary school. (Jimmy, parent)

Pupils may become the target of homophobic or biphobic bullying if they are connected to people who are lesbian, gay or bisexual. If they have parents of the same gender, a sibling or close friend who is lesbian, gay or bisexual these young people can face the same stigma attached to being gay. Once again, this may cause negative messages and stereotypes about their family or friends to become internalised. This makes it difficult to associate with people who are lesbian, gay or bisexual due to 'guilt by association'. In Jimmy's case, this is demonstrated by his son's unwillingness to be picked up from school.

Young people experiencing bullying because of their connection to people who are lesbian, gay or bisexual are also less likely to report it. This can be because they are scared that if they report it they too will be labelled as such. It can also be that they do not want to upset the friend or family member concerned. Parents who have a child who is being bullied will always find this a distressing experience. For same-sex parents, this can place an additional strain as homophobic bullying has historically been used to undermine the validity of lesbian or gay parenting.

It is not at all uncommon for homophobic or biphobic bullying to start in primary school. Children and young people's ideas about what is and is not acceptable regarding sexuality form from a very early age. While most children in primary school will not fully understand what homophobic language means its use communicates strong messages about what is acceptable behaviour. Too few primary schools have received training or support to address homophobic and biphobic bullying robustly and may not always be aware of the role it is playing in children's bullying. Ofsted's guidance on preventing homophobic bullying requires primary schools to challenge pupils who use 'gay' pejoratively and explain why it is wrong, address bullying where pupils are picked on for not behaving like a 'typical girl' or 'typical boy' and ensure that pupils are taught about different families (Ofsted, 2014a).

> I had a friend at this school who tried to write a letter to Disney because there are no gay princesses and they're all really stereotypical and need saving. Why can't they save themselves? They run off and marry a prince. Why can't they marry a princess? (Cola, 13)

The 2019 Ofsted inspection framework means that schools who fail to tackle bullying will be penalised in their ratings (see Box 2.1).

Box 2.1: Ofsted inspection guidelines 2019

Ofsted inspectors will assess the extent to which your school complies with the relevant legal duties as set out in the Equality Act 2010, including, where relevant, the Public Sector Equality Duty 2011 and the Human Rights Act 1998.

Schools must prepare learners for life in modern Britain by equipping them to be responsible, respectful, active citizens who contribute positively to society and by developing their understanding and appreciation of diversity – celebrating what we have in common and promoting respect for the different protected characteristics as defined in law. This includes LGBT groups.

In practice, this means that relationships among learners and staff should reflect a positive and respectful culture. Leaders, teachers and learners create an environment where bullying, peer-on-peer abuse or discrimination are not tolerated. If they do occur, staff must deal with issues quickly and effectively and not allow them to spread. Furthermore, leaders must protect their staff from bullying and harassment.

Adapted from Ofsted's Inspection Framework, 2019

'Suspected' of being lesbian, gay or bisexual

I'm 16 years old and mostly hang out with girls rather than boys. I feel safer when I'm with a group of girls and there is less pressure to play sport and be aggressive. The bullying started when I was 13 as everyone said I had a 'gay voice'. Last year a classmate accused me of being gay. Now everyone has got it into their heads that I am. (Ryan, 16)

Pupils can be 'suspected' of being lesbian, gay or bisexual for a number of reasons. Often this has a lot to do with expectations around gender and gender roles. For boys, the pressure can be to behave in an aggressive, 'macho' manner and position themselves in opposition to girls or gay men. Therefore in Ryan's case, the strong association with girls and his disinterest in sport and aggression cast 'suspicion' on his sexuality. In other cases, challenging the homophobia of other pupils can cause one to become a target.

'Oh, are you gay too?' is what happens if we challenge homophobia. It should be the teachers who do it. (Jack, 14)

Being bullied because people assume you are gay can be just as damaging to young people as being bullied because you are lesbian, gay or bisexual. Young people may be less likely to report this type of bullying for fear of confirming the bullies' accusations. Sometimes when young people are courageous enough to report it they are met with the response, 'If you're not gay, what is the problem?' As a result, the homophobic or biphobic element of the bullying may not be dealt with effectively or at all.

Homophobic and biphobic bullying as proxy

I'm 15 years old and Sikh. I've never experienced any abuse because of my background before but recently I have been having problems. I do not shave because of my religion and every time I get ready for PE class this girl clique call me a 'hairy dyke'. My friends have offered to shave my legs for me but I don't want to give in to the pressure of a small group of girls. (Aagya, 15)

Young people will experience homophobic or biphobic bullying differently depending on a range of factors, including gender, sexual orientation, class, faith, ethnicity and disability. In Aagya's case, she feels that homophobic language is being used to stigmatise her expression of faith. Educators should be aware that homophobic language can be used as a proxy for gendered, disablist or racist prejudice. A survey of 5032 young people's experiences online found that young carers and those with special educational needs experienced far higher rates of homophobic abuse online than their peers (Katz, 2013). This can often be because homophobic language is more common, less likely to be challenged and easier to 'get away with' than other forms of prejudice-driven language.

While the targeting of her faith appears to be Aagya's primary concern we should not assume that the homophobic element does not bother her. It is all too common for us not to consider the multiple identities of young people and particularly to presume heterosexuality among black, Asian and minority ethnic (BAME) and disabled young people. People who experience discrimination and abuse because of their faith, ethnicity or disability may be reluctant to disclose their sexual orientation as it becomes an additional issue with which to deal. Either way, it is important in cases such as Aagya's that both prejudiced attitudes are addressed and the young people involved understand that prejudice-based bullying of any kind will not be tolerated.

> We need to give pupils more opportunities to secure support from a number of teachers – not just one. There are lots of pupils facing trauma and we need to support them. (Ari, 14)

A lot of lesbian, gay or bisexual young people tell a teacher, youth worker or other adult in a position of trust before they tell a parent that they are, or think they are, gay. This calls on that adult's full duty of care, sense of responsibility and diplomacy skills if and when it comes to negotiating communications or liaisons between home and this young person.

It is vital to hold on to the fact that coming out as gay, lesbian or bisexual at school can mean having precious few people to turn to for genuine, committed support. Pupils who can confide in understanding, caring friends are the young people you may not get to hear about except when the subject is discussed casually in your presence. Many pupils experience bullying in school so when bullying accompanies coming out it is a double-edged sword: a young person needs support when coming out but often is reluctant to report homophobic or biphobic bullying. This is explored in Chapter 8.

It is not only pupils targeted by homophobic or biphobic bullying who may be struggling with coming out or their perceived sexual orientation. Chapter 3 highlights the characteristics of pupils who engage in homophobic bullying and the transience of labels such as 'bully' and 'victim', noting that young people can be both the 'bully' and the 'victim' throughout their school experience

KEY POINTS

✓ Homophobic name-calling can start as early as primary school.

✓ Homophobic and biphobic bullying affects heterosexual pupils and those yet to know their sexuality.

✓ Primary schools invariably meet the issue of homophobic or biphobic bullying when one of their pupils (aged around ten)

experiences homophobic bullying because they have 'two mums'. Homophobia and biphobia do not begin and end in our secondary schools.

✓ Young people will experience homophobic and biphobic bullying differently depending on a range of factors, including gender, sexual orientation, class, faith, ethnicity and disability.

CHAPTER 3

Who Perpetuates Homophobic and Biphobic Bullying?

Just as there is no one 'type' of person who experiences homophobic or biphobic bullying there is no single 'type' of its perpetrator. Pupils from all kinds of backgrounds can engage in this prejudice-driven behaviour. They may attempt justification of their actions for a number of reasons and these are explored in more detail in Chapter 4. Explored in this chapter are common factors which have been assigned to perpetrators of homophobic and biphobic bullying. These are identified not to create a discrete and distinct profile of a 'bully' but to gain a better understanding of what may cause someone to behave in this way.

While we may discuss bullying in terms that categorise pupils into different roles – the perpetrator, the target or the bystander – it is important to recognise that these roles are not fixed. Pupils who have been bullied may engage in bullying themselves as a form of retaliation. Similarly, a pupil can be a bystander in one incident but a perpetrator or target in another. In addition, pupils who engage in face-to-face bullying can differ greatly from those who perpetrate abuse online. As a result the distinction between a bully, a target and a bystander is rarely clear cut.

Research into bullying has indicated that both those who perpetrate and those who experience bullying share a number of common difficulties which can explain why they are involved in the experience. These include 'internalised distress' such as anxiety, depression, low self-esteem, academic problems and difficulty making friends, and 'externalised distress' such as anger, oppositional behaviour and poor impulse control (Nansel *et al.*, 2001). Both those who bully and those who are targeted can have difficulties responding to stress and coping with conflict in peer relationships. While young people who bully do report the internalising of problems it is much more common for them to exhibit externalising behaviour. In other words, in response to stress some young people may act out while others withdraw.

Ultimately there is no steadfast rule as to why a pupil may bully someone. Looking specifically at homophobic and biphobic bullying we can identify some potential stress factors that contribute to a perpetrator's experience of this type of bullying. Once again, factors can overlap with those perpetrating homophobic or biphobic bullying actually doing so because of another aspect of their identity: religion, disability or culture for example.

Sexual orientation

We rarely question the sexual orientation of those who perpetrate homophobic or biphobic bullying. Much as it is often presumed that someone experiencing homophobic bullying is lesbian, gay or bisexual, we can wrongly assume perpetrators are always heterosexual. Many young people who engage in this type of bullying behaviour will be doing so before they are confident of their own sexual orientation. Whether these young people are lesbian, gay, bisexual or heterosexual, homophobia and biphobia are tied up with the perpetrator's understanding and expression of their own sexual orientation.

I think a lot of people who are homophobic are worried they're gay. (Elsie, 13)

Young people who distance themselves from lesbian, gay or bisexual people through homophobia can be just as much trying to affirm their identity as the girl or the boy society expects them to be, so as to 'prove' their sexual orientation.

Young people grow up familiar with the stigmas attached to being lesbian, gay or bisexual. The negativity surrounding these identities can lead to a conscious or unconscious desire to be seen as heterosexual whether they have a genuine comprehension of their sexual orientation or not. The expression of heterosexuality in some young people often involves distancing themselves from and denigrating anything or anyone perceived to be gay. It is not simply enough to know you are heterosexual you have to 'prove it' through expected behaviours and rituals which can include homophobic and biphobic bullying and certainly homophobic language: however mild.

Homophobic bullying is an expression of insecurity among hetero-sexual, lesbian, gay and bisexual young people alike. Heterosexuality continues to occupy dominant status throughout the world and heterosexual young people can fear that they will lose the social advantage that this identity affords them. Homophobia and biphobia perpetrated by lesbian, gay or bisexual young people can be a result of internalised homophobia. All young people are exposed to negative messages about gay identities and this can influence lesbian, gay and bisexual pupils' understandings of their own sexuality. This can result in the denial of their sexual orientation, feelings of inadequacy, low self-esteem or contempt for those who are out as or are perceived to be gay.

When one's standing in the world and the opportunities available are dictated by whether we love people of the same gender, the insecurity this creates can be oppressive. The stigma attached to being lesbian, gay or bisexual does not just affect those who belong to those groups but fosters insecurity among heterosexual young people too – obliged as they are to present themselves in ways 'appropriate' to their gender (and being 'appropriately' gendered means one is heterosexual).

When heterosexual, lesbian, gay and bisexual identities are truly valued as equal we find that homophobic and biphobic attitudes and behaviours fall away. No longer is one required to push others down in order to pull oneself up. We are all valued and we are all equal.

Gender

Sexual orientation is not the only factor that can place pressure on young people to behave in certain ways. Just as sexual orientation prescribes our position in society, so does gender. Individuals are expected to adopt the gender roles (masculine or feminine) deemed socially acceptable to their sex (male or female) (see Box 3.1). Boys are often expected to be aggressors who experience and perpetrate physical bullying, verbal abuse and vandalism whereas girls are associated with relational bullying such as excluding others or rumour-mongering. With homophobic and biphobic bullying, we also tend to find that boys rather than girls are more commonly both the perpetrators and the victims. The sex of a young person (whether they are male or female) however does not predetermine whether they will engage in bullying or not. Instead it is the gendered expectations we place on boys and girls which determine this.

The expectations of femininity placed on girls can mean that physical behaviour and direct aggression are discouraged as 'unladylike'. As a result, less directly confrontational behaviour is common such as ostracism and gossip. For boys however physical aggression is a socially acceptable masculine trait and can be dismissed by educators as simply 'boys being boys'. When the roles are reversed with, for instance, girls exhibiting overt physical aggression and boys gossiping schools can stigmatise this behaviour as exceptionally problematic. In such situations our response to the bullying may not only denigrate what the perpetrator did but also denigrate them for not behaving as a 'typical girl' or 'typical boy'.

> From a young age, you're told you're a girl: you're expected to do this or that and go play with the princess dolls in the corner. That's what's expected of you. They don't expect you to break the gender norms and roles. I remember being a kid and the girls all said, 'I want to dance' or do this or that and one kid said, 'I want to be a racing driver' and then someone told them, 'You can't do that, you're a girl' and it's like you're expected to follow this pattern that everyone has laid out for you. (Ria, 15)

The pressure to conform to gender expectations can cause a great deal of anxiety among young people. Boys feel at a disadvantage if they are seen as weak or effeminate and girls risk exclusion or abuse if they do not invest in a 'feminine' presentation. This anxiety can lead to misogynistic, homophobic and biphobic bullying. The stigma attached to being lesbian, gay or bisexual is not solely about the dislike of such relationships but the fact that gay men are culturally aligned with femininity while lesbian women are culturally aligned with masculinity. Common homophobic insults additionally include those which imply or state that lesbian women are simply not 'attractive enough' to date men, or boys are gay because they did not have a 'strong father figure'. In order to be a 'proper boy' or a 'proper girl' you must be heterosexual and act 'appropriately' for your gender.

This stigma around sexuality can be just as much about gender and sexism as it is about homophobia. It is important to recognise how these issues relate to one another so that both can be challenged. Once again, in settings where boys and girls are viewed as equals and the gender behaviours available to them are flexible and numerous you will find less homophobic and biphobic bullying.

Box 3.1: Sex and gender

Sex is used to refer to the biological characteristics which define bodies as male or female. Gender however is used to refer to socially constructed roles and attributes that a given society considers appropriate for boys and men or girls and women. Invariably, features defining sex will be shared across different human societies while the defining features of gender differ greatly around the world. Some also draw the distinction that sex is biological while gender refers to the social groups of men and women, boys and girls.

Much work has been undertaken exploring the differences between sex and gender and the above description is not prescriptive. It is important to understand however that the behaviours deemed appropriate for individuals are not absolute or uninfluenced by cultural and social factors. Too often we use gender to place a moral judgement on those who do not conform to our expectations.

Individuals who fail to conform to the gendered expectations placed on them by society are socially penalised. Since heterosexuality is considered an essential part of 'properly' performing one's gender lesbian, gay and bisexual people are often the targets of this kind of social disapproval. Heterosexual, bisexual and gay men who are seen to reject traditional masculine gender roles in other ways can experience this discrimination too. Unsatisfactorily embodying masculinity can cause boys and men to be considered effeminate and, due to sexist attitudes within society, femininity is culturally degraded. In this way homophobia is closely aligned with misogyny. Heterosexual, bisexual and lesbian women who present with traits traditionally deemed masculine are often viewed as 'unnatural' and threatening.

Age

Homophobic and biphobic bullying can be perpetrated by people of all ages. We tend to associate the problem with pupils in secondary school. It can begin in our primary schools however and continue into college, university or the workplace. Pupils who continue to perpetrate homophobic or biphobic abuse after they leave school are likely to be penalised: losing jobs, positions at university or even finding themselves guilty of prejudice-based crime (hate crime). It is important therefore that this behaviour is challenged as early as possible.

It is only recently that the importance of addressing homophobic and biphobic bullying in primary school has been embraced. I had a primary school teacher say to me at a conference at which I had been invited to speak about challenging homophobic and biphobic bullying in primary and secondary schools that she thought that this topic was 'Really more a big school issue…'. When a teacher describes secondary school as big school we can see easily why we so often end up placing a sticking plaster over the symptoms of homophobia and biphobia in our secondary schools: expressly because too few of our primary school colleagues recognise the vital role they play in educating children (and each other) about the need to introduce children to an awareness of different families and children's various home circumstances and to look at diversity through more than simply the lens of race, ethnicity or disability.

While Years 7–11 (ages 12–16) are those where we most commonly see homophobic and biphobic bullying it tends to decrease in sixth form (ages 16–18). More people are openly lesbian, gay or bisexual here – and it is interesting to note that teachers tell me regularly that pupils who are 'out' will frequently experience less bullying than their peers whom others perceive to be lesbian, gay or bisexual. I have also found that gay, lesbian and bisexual teachers in sixth-form settings are more likely to be 'out' to their A-level students. Interestingly, this is tacitly appealing to their sixth formers' maturity not to blab to the younger years the fact that their teachers are gay. Years 7–11 often remain in blissful ignorance of gay teachers in their school and regrettably we still see a dearth of thriving, successful, positive 'out' lesbian, gay and bisexual role models in the teaching profession.

Disability

The experiences of pupils with disabilities or additional needs can often be overlooked. EACH and other organisations regularly receive enquiries from teachers (seeking support or staff training) who work with pupils with additional needs. Pupils with, for example, autism or Asperger syndrome can fail to recognise the impact homophobic and biphobic classroom insults can have on their peers. Sometimes pupils will simply be expressing legitimate curiosity about differences but without the understanding to utilise appropriate language. Most insults are brought in from home and elder siblings but teachers often express exasperation at how racist or homophobic parents can be which makes educating children with additional needs that much harder. At other times, pupils may be lashing out at others and targeting differences as an expression of personal frustration.

My parents make homophobic comments all the time. (Adam, 14)

It is important to remember that post-pubertal pupils with additional needs have a sexuality just as mainstream school youngsters do. Teachers often voice concerns to EACH as to whether they are granting enough attention to the pupils in their school who may be struggling to understand or come to terms with their evolving sexuality – especially when this is lesbian, gay or bisexual. It is essential to bear in mind also that a significant minority of young people with additional needs will also be lesbian, gay or bisexual.

Ethnicity

Everyone has an 'ethnicity' and shares common national or cultural traditions with others. In England and Wales the majority of the population is White British. We also have a rich cultural history of ethnic diversity with a large White Irish, Asian British, Black African and Black Caribbean population as well as many people from across Europe, the Middle East and the Americas (Office for National Statistics, 2019). Many people will share multiple and sometimes conflicting national or cultural traditions depending on their ethnicity. This can be particularly evident in young people who will have lived in the UK all their life but whose parents or grandparents grew up outside it.

While it is important not to stereotype any group we must recognise that views on sexual orientation and gender identity will vary and mean different things within different cultures. While some cultures celebrate and revere diversity of sexuality and gender identity there are many which are not as inclusive or tolerant (see Box 3.2). For young people who come from, or whose parents come from, countries where being lesbian, gay or bisexual is considered 'deviant', their attitude towards such relationships is more likely to be at best more conservative (and at worst openly hostile) than those from countries which value those relationships.

Box 3.2: Being gay around the world

Dozens of countries around the world continue to outlaw same-sex relationships and persecute and prosecute people for being lesbian, gay or bisexual. In Iran, Mauritania, Saudi Arabia, Sudan and Yemen being gay is punishable with the death penalty and in many other countries gay and lesbian people face imprisonment. Even in nations where same-sex relationships are not illegal lesbian and gay people are still denied equal rights and experience unequal ages of consent or marriage bans.

The UK often prides itself on its progressive track record (particularly in the last decade) towards equal rights for lesbian and gay people. It should not be forgotten however that anti-gay laws in many countries around the world are the legacy of British colonial rule.

Coming from a family background with strong views against same-sex relationships can lead pupils to engage in homophobic or biphobic bullying. If a young person has been taught that these relationships are wrong they may express this through bullying behaviours which target anyone who is or is perceived to be lesbian, gay or bisexual. These young people can also struggle with intense internalised homophobia if they are gay. While positive visibility within the media, education and wider society is poor for all gay people, it is exceptionally lacking for those from an ethnic minority background. This erasure of black, Asian and ethnic minority lesbian, gay and bisexual people creates a commonly held misconception that 'all gay young people are white'. This can lead us to overlook the experiences of those from different ethnicities and even anticipate or ignore homophobia or biphobia because of their cultural background.

Regardless of ethnicity or cultural background, there are plenty of adults who hold on to prejudices and pass these on to their children. When a person's justification for their prejudice is related to their national or cultural identity teachers can feel less confident about challenging such attitudes. After all, it is easier to challenge someone with whom you perceive a shared national or cultural tradition than it is to challenge someone whose culture you know or understand little about. Despite this, there is a strong legal and moral imperative for us all to challenge homophobia and biphobia whenever it occurs just as there is an imperative to challenge racism or disablism wherever this occurs.

While these issues may sometimes seem in conflict they should be considered in unison. Respect for equality and diversity does not work if it is applied to only one 'issue' or constituency of interest. Educating young people about respecting and celebrating our national or cultural differences can be a great platform for recognising and celebrating all kinds of different families, relationships and so on. After all, respect, empathy and kindness are transferable skills.

> Equality isn't a finite resource with there being only so much to go around. (Rachel Lowrie, Key Stage 3 Leader of Learning for English, Churchill Academy & Sixth Form, North Somerset)

Faith

In many ways, the homophobic attitudes manifested by some with strong religious convictions look largely similar to those whose national identity is used as a justification for their prejudice. The value that different nations place on sexual orientation is often underpinned by religious belief, and religion shapes many cultures around the world.

Religion can be a divisive topic, particularly when discussed in relation to sexuality. For some, religion is about peace, love, comfort and community while for others it calls to mind sectarianism, war, hate and narrow-mindedness. Faith is frequently used as a justification for homophobic prejudice as evidenced by debates in the UK about equal marriage rights and changes to the RSE curriculum. As a result, discussions of lesbian, gay and bisexual equality and religious freedom can often be seen to be in competition with one another. Religion encompasses a multitude of beliefs however and is not synonymous with homophobic or biphobic prejudice.

Great Britain is today a largely secular society. Although Christianity remains its largest religion, fewer and fewer people are identifying as Christian each census. At the same time, there has been a rise in the number of people identifying as Muslim, Buddhist, Hindu or Jewish and almost 37 per cent of the population in England report having no religion (Office for National Statistics, 2019). Great Britain is not however, a secular state and religion still plays an important part in our school system. In England and Wales around a third of all state-funded schools are those 'with a religious character' (Department for Education, 2017b). The vast majority are Church of England, but schools 'with a religious character' also include Roman Catholic, Jewish, Muslim and Greek Orthodox among other religions.

The role of religion within the British school system is not without controversy. People of all faiths and no faith are critical of religious schools' right to discriminate in selection and recruitment to favour pupils from a particular religious background. In 2014, a number of Muslim majority schools in Birmingham, UK, were embroiled in four separate investigations examining claims that hard-line extremists were 'trying to take control'. The investigations into alleged extremism in some Birmingham schools were sparked by assertions of gender discrimination, homophobia, extremist views, bullying and unfair employment practices.

Similar concerns were raised in 2012 when Catholic schools were found to be distributing a pamphlet entitled 'Pure Manhood: How to become the man God wants you to be' which featured homophobic commentary and undermined HIV prevention campaigns. Further controversy followed later in the year when the Catholic Education Service wrote to all state-funded Roman Catholic secondary schools in England and Wales highlighting that it was every Catholic's duty to oppose equal marriage for lesbian and gay people.

Cases such as these and the accompanying media frenzy can undermine public trust in schools with a religious character and their ability to promote a safe learning environment for all. The Department for Education said it takes action if there are any concerns that a school is not meeting the independent schools' standards. Of course, some faith schools will be liberal in their attitude to equality and diversity while others will be at the other end of the continuum. Prejudice-based bullying can too easily thrive in extreme circumstances. What is important as far as any pupil is concerned is that religious convictions do not allow, foster or promulgate bullying of any kind.

Throughout 2019, two Birmingham primary schools were targeted by protests coordinated by adults unhappy with the inclusion of LGBT issues on the school curriculum. These adults, who were mostly Muslim in faith (some were also of other religions), found that teaching children that it's 'okay to be gay' was in conflict with their beliefs. At one point, a gathering of 300 protestors caused one of the schools to close early (Johnston, 2019). The protestors claimed that since the areas surrounding the primary schools are almost entirely made up of Muslim residents teaching should reflect this and thus any mention of LGBT issues or gay and lesbian relationships should be excluded. As Russell Hobby, head of Teach First and former general secretary of the National Association of Head Teachers wrote in *The Guardian* newspaper:

> No parent has a right to restrict their children from learning about other safe and legal values and other perspectives on the world. Not restricting knowledge seems to me to be the best criteria for balancing the rights of parents, young people and society as a whole. (Hobby, 2019)

Parents have a right to teach their child their own values and belief system as they see fit but the introduction of statutory RSE and PSHE in schools reduces parents' ability to *control* what their child learns about the world and other people. Furthermore, in November 2019 a high court judge banned the protests outside one Birmingham school stating that the protest exposed the children to far more sexualised language than they would have met through teaching (Lyons, 2019). As all schools are obliged to teach topics such as LGBT issues there will be an increased likelihood that some parents will take issue with the curriculum. In making the curriculum compulsory however rather than 'at the discretion' of the school it may be easier to remove personal responsibility from schools and individual teachers and make it clear to parents that even if they chose to remove their children from sex education they cannot prevent children being taught about diverse family types, LGBT issues, or that it is in fact 'okay to be gay'. For information on the new statutory Relationships and Sex Education curriculum and advice to schools facing protests please see Appendices 2 and 3 respectively.

There are, fortunately, many examples of schools with a religious character, or serving a largely religious constituency, fostering a deep commitment to equality, civil rights and the promotion of mutual understanding. EACH and other similar organisations have worked with many faith schools as well as religious young people to prevent homophobic bullying within their settings. These schools and their pupils feel that the use of religion to justify homophobic oppression belittles their faith and they possess a conviction to challenge this and do so for instance through films for schools they have produced with EACH.

Indeed, EACH consulted closely with the Church of England, its staff and ministers in the lead up to its creation of *Valuing All God's Children:*

Guidance for Church of England Schools on Challenging Homophobic Bullying (Church of England Archbishops' Council Education Division, 2014; revised 2019). This is a major step forward in the Church's efforts to endorse same-sex relationships and condemn homophobic and biphobic bullying.

Religious education (RE) has an important role to play in promoting social cohesion and the values of respect and empathy. It is a legal requirement to provide pupils with a broad religious education. Ofsted has argued that the full potential of RE is not being realised in many schools (Ofsted, 2013). Effective RE places enquiry at the heart of learning, engages pupils in 'big questions', enables them to reconsider their positions, investigate religions and explore new possibilities (Ofsted, 2013). RE provides a great opportunity to teach pupils about a range of religious and cultural perspectives surrounding matters of sexual diversity and gender and challenge some taken-for-granted assumptions. The 2019 Ofsted framework examines the extent to which religious education develops pupils' ability to be reflective about their own beliefs (religious or otherwise) and perspective on life (Ofsted, 2019).

Chapter 4 explores some of these taken-for-granted assumptions and develops a broader understanding of the beliefs that underlie homophobic bullying and how some young people attempt to justify this behaviour.

KEY POINTS

✓ Homophobic and biphobic bullying should be challenged from primary school onwards.

✓ Perpetrators of homophobic and biphobic bullying can be heterosexual, lesbian, gay, bisexual or simply unsure of their sexuality.

✓ Be wary of reinforcing gender stereotypes when challenging homophobic and biphobic bullying.

✓ Anti-homophobic and biphobic bullying work complements wider equality and diversity work challenging racist, faith-based, disablist and other prejudice-based bullying.

✓ Religious convictions should in no circumstances be used as a justification for allowing or excusing homophobic or biphobic bullying.

CHAPTER 4

Why Do Young People Bully Homophobically or Biphobically?

EACH has worked with over 15,000 young people to date exploring their experiences and understanding of homophobia, biphobia, transphobia, sexism and cyberbullying. Targets, bystanders and perpetrators have all engaged with EACH's services over the years. Listening to the wide-ranging voices of young people has led to a broad understanding of the reasons young people bully homophobically and biphobically. Some common justifications and scenarios are explored in detail below.

> I have clashes with one bully all the time. He just doesn't listen. You can tell him over and over again that what he's saying isn't okay but he won't listen to you, he'll just ignore you. At the end of the day, it comes down to his religious belief that being gay is a problem. (Ria, 16)

The fact remains that many people still believe that lesbian, gay and bisexual people are 'wrong', 'unnatural' or do not deserve equal rights. These sentiments can too easily be echoed by others, especially when lack of life experience or a limited exposure to diversity in the wider world has allowed them to form negative assumptions about lesbian, gay and bisexual people. As in Ria's example, some argue that their religion says it is wrong to be gay. It is important to bear in mind the distinction between gay people being 'invisible' and being 'absent'. Lesbian, gay and bisexual people are ever present but rendered invisible by language, advertising, television, film and magazine portrayals. If you are not depicted you are, by default, voiceless, powerless, worthless. You only matter if you are counted and you are only counted if you matter. It is a self-fulfilling prophecy.

Prejudice usually involves viewing people as part of a group and assuming that everyone in this group is the same. People of all ages can have a very limited view of what lesbian, gay and bisexual people are really like – which is in reality extraordinarily like everyone else. Young people hear about sexuality from a variety of sources including family, friends, spokespeople representing their religion or the media. All too often myths and stereotypes abound based on overheard ridiculing expressed by adults (who often are in positions of social authority), older teenagers and elder siblings. Lack of life experience or exposure to diversity simply compounds ignorance and misinformation.

The coverage of England's equal marriage debate in 2013 illustrates this point. The media frequently gave voice to the views of those who compared same-sex marriage to incest and bestiality. We cannot take it for granted that young people will question these assertions and understand the dangers inherent within such opinions. Educators must engage proactively with topical debates such as equal marriage rights if they are to prevent young people from rehearsing these views and targeting their peers.

It is vitally important therefore that teachers and staff in all schools address issues of sexual orientation with pupils in their classes because the school system is a microcosm of society at large. Children need to be exposed to many different beliefs and opinions. Schools have the opportunity, and in fact the obligation, to prepare them for the outside world where they will work with adults who are lesbian, gay or bisexual. Pupils must be prepared to enter society with a more open mind, where all individuals deserve the right to be who they are, regardless of sexual orientation.

People see [homophobia] on TV or read things and this gets brought into school. (Britney, 14)

While not all young people or their teachers hold overtly homophobic views, some may unconsciously or otherwise maintain the belief that being heterosexual is 'normal' and right while being lesbian, gay or bisexual is inferior and less acceptable. Once again, this attitude is consistently reinforced through mainstream films, TV shows, advertising and magazines where being lesbian, gay or bisexual is represented as a source of anxiety, a threat, an object of amusement or abuse or simply not represented at all.

So, who has the problem? Teachers, especially those with strong religious convictions, struggling with 'out' gay teens but happy to see gay people as judges and competitors on *Strictly Come Dancing* or any number of game, chat or reality shows? The fact is that, for many of our pupils, it is media portrayals which are informing how they see lesbian, gay and bisexual people (see Box 4.1).

Box 4.1: Television shows influencing pupils' understanding of gay, lesbian and bisexual people

Queer Eye

Five gay and bisexual men who specialise in fashion, food and wine, grooming, culture and interior design go to the rescue of hapless individuals (mostly heterosexual men) with no sense of fashion or anything else and complete a makeover. The contestant is often a man who cannot cook, is culturally unsophisticated and oblivious about home décor. The hosts show them their perceptions of how to fix these problems pertaining to their corresponding specialisms.

The Circle

First aired in 2018, *The Circle* sees contestants living in the same house together – but communicating exclusively via social media. The contestants can choose to 'play' as themselves or to create a new identity. The most popular contestant at the end of the series wins the prize. The first two seasons of the show each featured LGBT contestants pretending to be heterosexual. The first series saw a gay man participating as a heterosexual woman and the second series a lesbian playing as a younger, heterosexual woman.

Friends

Despite retaining its popularity 25 years after it first aired, *Friends* has not aged well. The show frequently makes use of stereotypes about lesbian, gay and bisexual people and treats them as a punchline. The 'gay panic' of Chandler and his desperate attempts to prove his heterosexuality, frequent jokes made about Ross' ex-wife, who is a lesbian and the transphobic treatment of Chandler's mother are some of the long-term storylines that relied on homophobia and transphobia.

Rupaul's Drag Race
Drag queens compete in various challenges to win the competition and the crown of 'America's Next Drag Superstar'. A UK version of the show aired in 2019. The challenges span comedy, fashion, acting and dancing. With a few exceptions the show features feminine, stereotypically 'bitchy' drag queens. In addition to some heartfelt moments there is an awful lot of drama and many unhelpful stereotypes are reinforced.

The Circle follows a lineage of reality TV shows which exploit the idea of 'playing it straight'. This is damaging because it aligns lesbian, gay and bisexual people with deception and suggests that they can 'choose' to stop being gay. It also adds to the stigma that suggests one cannot exceed or get ahead (or win a popularity competition) if they are out as lesbian, gay or bisexual. This is a damaging and dangerous message to send to anyone who is beginning to understand their sexuality in the face of already difficult stigma.

The camp comedy of *RuPaul's Drag Race* and the hyper-fashionable, hyper-stylised *Queer Eye* 'Fab Five' are not alone necessarily problematic but in the absence of more varied representation it can be hard for young people to construct ideas of gay, lesbian and bisexual people that do not rely heavily on stereotypes. The exploitation of stereotypes in television presentations of gay men has a long history which manifests itself in the media that pupils consume today. It is useful therefore to explore this history in order to understand and challenge homophobic stereotypes in today's media.

For example, *Little Britain's* Daffyd ('the only gay in the village') was a reincarnation of Dick Emery's 1970s effeminate gay male character Clarence, also known as Honky Tonks. As Laurence Marcus observes in *Clever Dick: Dick Emery's Comic Creations* (Marcus, 2019):

Emery stated that adopting a camp attitude was a useful ploy when faced with an unresponsive audience. 'Why the suggestion of homosexuality should be funny is imponderable – perhaps our laughter is defence, a reaction against hidden fears about our innermost tendencies', he contemplated. By the 1970s, gay characters appeared more openly although they were portrayed as farcical and camp and created purely for comic relief. At the same time as

Clarence became a staple of Emery's repertoire, John Inman was starring on television as Grace Brothers' decidedly effeminate (but undeclared homosexual [sic]) menswear salesman Mr. Humphries in *Are You Being Served?* and Larry Grayson was making a name for himself camping it up as the comedian with a decidedly gay persona which actually formed the mainstay of his act. Clarence was probably the template for *Little Britain*'s Daffyd and one imagines that Matt Lucas has taken the character and shown us his modern-day version. In the early 1970s, Clarence was the only gay in the village.

Interviewer: Excuse me, sir.

Clarence: Oh, hello Honky Tonks, how are you?

Interviewer: I'm asking questions about class distinction.

Clarence: Oh, yes?

Interviewer: Do you believe there's an 'us' and a 'them'?

Clarence: Well, it doesn't bother me really – I'm one of those!

People's attitudes change when someone comes out. We need lessons on this to help teachers help pupils understand how to constructively respond to others. They need to communicate to pupils that being gay is just like being heterosexual and only a little bit different. We need to normalise. (Mai, 15)

Stereotype busting is needed. (Ava, 14)

Box 4.2 contains a useful activity for exploring stereotypes about lesbian, gay and bisexual people with your pupils. Although young people who hold on to stereotypes may not wish to withhold equal rights from gay people they may well have their sense of who lesbian, gay and bisexual people 'are' skewed by television depictions and not see rights as a priority or empathise with the issue. As a result, they can unknowingly perpetrate homophobia and biphobia themselves through taunting which they will call 'banter' or be complicit bystanders when name-calling turns into homophobic or biphobic bullying.

The belief that being lesbian, gay or bisexual is inferior to being heterosexual leads to subtle behaviours such as jokes and vocabulary that can be very damaging to young people. One of the most obvious examples is the pejorative use of the word 'gay' among young people to describe something as worthless, wrong, dull, stupid or rubbish. This use of language does not always constitute homophobic bullying as it is often targeted at objects and situations rather than individuals. It does however, function as a micro-aggression which elevates heterosexuality above lesbian, gay and bisexual identities making the latter synonymous with the dysfunctional, the inept and the undesirable (Aiden, Marston and Perry, 2013). It is the belief (held by some) that gay, lesbian and bisexual people are dysfunctional, unstable and contaminated (either mentally or physically) that feeds into many of the arguments against equal rights. If we continue to let these attitudes go unchallenged we risk damaging irrevocably the self-esteem and self-worth of all lesbian, gay and bisexual people.

Box 4.2: Lesbian, gay and bisexual visibility activity

Divide the class into small groups and ask each group to think of a famous lesbian, gay or bisexual person or character. On sticky notes they then write down traits of this person or character. After five to ten minutes invite pupils to feed back on the gay figure they were discussing and the traits they identified. Record the pupils' thoughts on the board and ask them to consider whether any of these traits are common to all lesbian, gay or bisexual people or to people in general.

Explain that people can sometimes assume that all lesbian, gay or bisexual people are alike for example that all gay men have great dress sense, all lesbians are butch or bisexual people cannot be monogamous. Highlight that these beliefs are stereotypes that are over-simplified, frequently untrue and can be very offensive.

Ask the pupils to identify any further stereotypes about gay people and discuss the following points:

- Where do we see/hear these stereotypes portrayed – for example in the news, on TV, in films or at school?

- What do the stereotypes have in common?

- Are any of the stereotypes funny? If so, why?

- How are these stereotypes dangerous or damaging?

- How do stereotypes affect the way we behave?

> • How can these stereotypes be challenged?
>
> Explain that stereotypes lead to prejudice and discrimination. The assumption that all lesbian, gay and bisexual people are alike leads to prejudice against them. It can also mean that the many gay people who do not fit these stereotypes feel invisible and voiceless.
>
> Adapted from EACH (2014)

The subtle reinforcement of heterosexual privilege does not start and end with 'That's so gay'. There are numerous ways in which the experiences of gay people can be trivialised and ridiculed. One simple example of this is the sale of t-shirts in foreign holiday resorts which read 'I think he's gay!' with an arrow pointing sideways or that read 'I'm not gay but £20 is £20!' It is astonishing that some online retailers in the UK have no problem with selling such t-shirts similarly. As in these cases, even the very words lesbian, gay and bisexual can be deployed as a cheap joke or insult. If pupils and indeed their teachers cannot adopt appropriate language without embarrassment it is problematic for creating an inclusive school culture. Once educators begin to have age-appropriate and open discussions with pupils about sexuality, pupils will be better prepared to discuss these topics appropriately and maturely. A prevailing issue concerning the discussion of sexuality in schools is a frequently conservative approach to RSE. Same-sex relationships are rarely discussed which not only puts the health and wellbeing of lesbian, gay and bisexual pupils at risk but also reinforces heterosexual privilege.

> The derogatory comments I recall from the earlier years are still with me now. If I'd been in Year 9 [13–14-year-olds] and seen an assembly about 'me' that said 'You're not wrong, it's not disgusting', that I wasn't dirty, it would have been so helpful. My school should have been a safe place but it wasn't. If a school normalises being gay that makes it more apparent to those who would make those comments that it's okay to be gay. It stops the 'cool' boys dropping those derogatory comments. Someone shouldn't have to find that pride themselves. (Linda, 17)
>
> [LGBT matters] are taught but it's just a lesson stating the facts… it isn't celebratory. There's no opportunity to find pride in yourself

in what's taught. There's no exploration of the past. Of history. (Malik, 16)

As pupils become more familiar with same-sex relationships within wider society questions about this aspect of lesbian, gay and bisexual lives will naturally arise. Yet too often the information to which pupils have access is inaccurate or generalised. This can lead to same-sex relationships becoming a source of mockery or derision. Once again, inclusive and age-appropriate conversations about same-sex relationships in RSE (see Appendix 2) will reinforce just how ordinary it is to be lesbian, gay or bisexual.

Many of our beliefs about what is normal and desirable are informed by gender and the way that certain behaviours, characteristics and qualities are culturally aligned with being a man or being a woman. Important in all of the work undertaken by EACH has been that with groups of young people exploring gender stereotyping and the pressures that they feel as boys or girls. Young people felt that girls are often judged by what they look like and wear while boys are often expected to be strong and interested in sport. It was also felt that when girls are interested in activities that boys are 'supposed to like' and boys are interested in activities girls are 'supposed to like' they can become the target of bullying.

Young people can feel the pressure to conform to these gendered ideas from a very young age in order to fit in and be popular. A report by the NSPCC in 2013 found that young people aged between 10 and 12 years of age spoke of feeling they were 'being pushed' into being a 'particular kind of "girl" or "boy"' (Renold, 2013, p.41).

From an early age, friendships between boys and girls are subject to romantic innuendo and platonic relationships between them can become stigmatised (Renold, 2013). The investment in boyfriend-girlfriend culture starts in primary school, quickly becoming a way in which children and young people establish and maintain status. In order to maintain this status, boys often feel they should define themselves in opposition to femininity. This manifests in boys distancing themselves from women or gay and bisexual men. Girls feel they should define themselves in opposition to masculinity and so similarly distance themselves from men and lesbian or bisexual women. This can lead to homophobic or biphobic abuse as young people seek to belittle behaviour that does not conform to their ideas of gender in order to assert their identity as a boy or a girl.

> As a little kid, you're very aware of your gender. I've got a six-year-old cousin who just started Year 1. So many times he's said to me, 'I'm a boy. I play football' and I'm just sitting there thinking, 'That's not how it works!' When I was his age I was into football, I was into racing, I was into all that kind of stuff. And even the teachers were like, 'Why don't you write about princesses, you know all of your friends know the names of the Disney princesses.' But that wasn't what I wanted to do. (Ria, 15)

In settings with decreasing incidents of homophobia one will often find an increase in the gendered behaviours open to boys and girls and more freedom of expression.

Schools will very rarely endorse overtly homophobic or biphobic behaviour and clear legislation should be in place to safeguard against this. Staff both in schools and other settings can nevertheless be complicit in reinforcing attitudes about the superiority of heterosexuality by rendering lesbian, gay and bisexual people invisible. Even where anti-bullying policies are in place (and individual incidents reported and dealt with) educational settings will struggle to challenge homophobic bullying effectively if underlying attitudes go unchallenged. While great work is being done to address homophobic bullying in many schools they often shy away from engaging young people in constructive and age-appropriate conversation about sexuality and instead treat it solely as a discipline issue.

> Punishments aren't the right way of going about it because there are those kids that don't care about getting punished, so it's not going to do anything, it just gives them satisfaction. We need to find another way to approach bullying. (Sky, 13)

It is not a surprise that schools are reluctant to discuss sexuality with their pupils when for 15 years they were strongly discouraged from doing so. Section 28 of the Local Government Act 1988 was one of the most pernicious pieces of anti-gay legislation in Britain, prohibiting local authorities from 'promoting the teaching in any maintained school of the acceptability of homosexuality as a pretended family relationship'. Since its repeal came into effect in Scotland on 21 June 2000 and then

England and Wales on 18 November 2003 we have seen a raft of legislative changes advancing the rights of lesbian, gay and bisexual people. From workplace protections, fostering and adoption rights, the introduction of civil partnerships, the introduction of same-sex marriage in England and Wales in 2014, in Scotland later that year and in Northern Ireland in 2019 – no longer can the relationships of lesbian, gay or bisexual people be dismissed as 'pretend', 'unacceptable' or illegitimate. Thirteen years after the repeal of Section 28, the 2020 RSE government guidelines make relationships education which includes families with lesbian, gay or bisexual parents compulsory in both primary and secondary schools (see Appendix 2 for more details).

While we might try to ameliorate the effects of bigotry in our schools some pupils come from homes that impart ignorance or intolerance. Other households do not foster openness and acceptance and many pupils come from homes where children and their parents have not been exposed to other cultures or minority groups. Some parents choose not to expose their children to diversity and others live in communities which lack it. School may be the only place where these pupils are exposed to cultures and people who are different from them.

If my years of supporting schools in challenging homophobia and biphobia have taught me anything it is that the cast of Section 28's shadow did not end in the year of its repeal in 2003. Although Section 28 was not even targeted at schools per se, many teachers are still too unconfident, unaware or sometimes too misinformed to address matters of sexual orientation beyond actual bullying matters. In 2013, 45 academies across Britain came under scrutiny as it was revealed that their Sex and Relationships Education policies included outdated Section 28-esque statements prohibiting the 'promotion of homosexuality'. This fear of 'promoting' lesbian, gay and bisexual issues has permeated school cultures for decades, effectively silencing constructive discussion about sexuality between pupils and teachers.

Sex Education Forum Young People's RSE Poll 2019

The Sex Education Forum ran a poll of 1000 young people aged 11–17 around England which asked them about their experiences of RSE in school and at home. The results found:

- Fewer than six in ten young people learned all they needed to

> at school about healthy relationships, abusive relationships, grooming and how to get help if they were sexually abused or assaulted.
>
> • Seventeen per cent of all respondents rate the quality of their school RSE as 'bad' or 'very bad'.
>
> • Eighteen per cent of young people learned nothing about LGBT issues at school and a further 28 per cent said they had not learned all that they needed to about LGBT issues.
>
> • Twenty-one per cent of young people learned nothing about LGBT issues at home and a further 31 per cent said they had not learned all that they needed to about LGBT issues.
>
> (Sex Education Forum, 2019)

As I have said previously, all too often addressing this topic comes down to a brave, sole teacher who has picked up the issue because they have someone in their personal life who is lesbian, gay or bisexual, they identify as such themselves or they are attempting to support a pupil. Over the years I have considered often how many lesbian, gay or bisexual teachers have entered the profession to 'make a difference' for the pupils in their schools, colleagues and ultimately society beyond imparting their subject matter knowledge. The fact that so many teachers feel affirmed only to be out to their colleagues or sixth formers says much about how confident they are to be their authentic, fully-rounded selves to everyone in their school – a privilege enjoyed by heterosexual teachers daily. This quote is from a teacher in Blaenau Gwent when I was delivering a staff training input at his school:

> I'd rather my 15-year-old son came home and told me he'd raped or murdered someone than told me he was gay.

Yes, he was appropriately disciplined.

In 2009, EACH was awarded Big Lottery funding to work with lesbian, gay, bisexual, transgender and heterosexual young people to challenge prejudice-based bullying. The five-year grant for EACH's Reach project enabled the charity to work with young people across Bristol, South Gloucestershire and North Somerset to create a practical toolkit for teachers and put young people's voices at the heart of work challenging homophobic, biphobic, transphobic and sexist bullying and cyberbullying. You may think it difficult to find fault with such an investment. The announcement of this funding in August 2009 however was denounced by the then leader of the Bristol Conservatives, Councillor Richard Eddy as a 'mistaken and misguided, outrageous waste of money' (Webster, 2009). The criticism was buoyed by a front-page spread from the *Bristol Evening Post* asking, 'So you call this equality?' (Webster, 2009). Both challenged the award for funding a minority issue and singling out gay young people for 'special treatment' (Webster, 2009).

To privileged people equality can feel like oppression. (Will, 16)

The so-called 'privileging' of minority groups for preferential treatment is a common criticism waged against equalities initiatives. What critics ignore is that those in the majority enjoy an invisible, privileged social status on a daily basis. This privilege freely rewards those in the majority with health, education, safety, security, recognition and numerous other basic rights. For those in the minority, such rights are hard won. Too often, lesbian, gay and bisexual young people are denied the opportunity to thrive, realise their academic and social potential and engage positively in all aspects of life. It is for this reason that EACH set about working with local lesbian, gay, bisexual, transgender and heterosexual young people on initiatives which strive to build confidence in the very institutions set up to nurture them.

Having previously co-authored *Safe to Learn: Homophobic Bullying* for the Department for Children, Schools and Families (2007), EACH (2014) went on to create the *Reach Teaching Resource*, a DVD of 13 short films with lesson plans. EACH was subsequently commissioned by the Department for Education to devise and deliver its own programme of work and assist Barnardo's with the delivery of its own initiative. EACH (2016) created the training and resource programme *Inspiring Equality in Education* and with the National Children's Bureau (2018), *Learn Equality, Live Equal.*

In 2019, EACH was commissioned to co-develop the Welsh Government's (2019) new statutory anti-bullying guidance, *Rights, Respect, Equality: Guidance for Schools*. Designed in close consultation with young people, the different resources resulting from these programmes open up a dialogue with pupils and teachers concerning prejudice-based bullying and cyberbullying. They are designed to prompt reflection on pupils' experiences, values and existing knowledge to meaningfully challenge prejudice-based bullying.

What we find when we have constructive and age-appropriate conversations with young people is that they share a greater understanding of rights, respect and equality than for which we give them credit. This allows them to express their views on what it means to be lesbian, gay or bisexual in society today. Young people recognise that while great progress has been made the terrible oppression suffered by gay people is part of our history and we are not all equal. We still live in a society where:

- about three-quarters of LGBT young people have experienced name-calling, nearly half have experienced harassment or threats and intimidation and almost a quarter have experienced physical assault (METRO Youth Chances, 2016)

- such abuse is portrayed as an inevitability of lesbian, gay and bisexual lives rather than a symptom of others' ignorance and prejudice

- support and guidance has to be sought out by lesbian, gay and bisexual young people rather than offered. Phrases such as 'That's so gay' reinforce feelings of isolation, insecurity and hostility on a daily basis.

There has been some progress in the inclusion of lesbian, gay and bisexual matters in the National Curriculum since the first version of this book was published in 2015. As of 2020, Relationships and Sex Education is a statutory subject in all schools in England (see Appendix 2 for a summary). The guidelines for its provision explicitly state that pupils are to be taught about different kinds of families, including families that include lesbian or gay parents, and that all teaching must comply with the 2010 Equality Act. RSE should also tackle the harmful nature of stereotypes and bullying in both primary and secondary schools. PSHE is compulsory in all schools from 2020 onwards. Furthermore, Ofsted made challenging bullying (including homophobic and biphobic bullying) and the provision of effective RSE key tenants of its 2019 Inspection Framework (Ofsted, 2019).

This new legislation necessitates that schools put in place strategies to improve their ability to challenge homophobic bullying and consulting with EACH or other training organisations can help your school here.

Schools have a legal as well as moral duty to protect children from homophobic and biphobic bullying. The 2011 Public Sector Equality Duty, part of the Equality Act 2010 (UK Government, 2010), requires that public bodies – including state, academy and free schools – must 'consider all individuals when carrying out their day-to-day work – in shaping policy, in delivering services and in relation to their own employees' (Government Equalities Office, 2011, p.3). Schools whose policies and practices are seen to discriminate against or disadvantage members of the pupil body are vulnerable to complaints of unlawful treatment. If schools are to truly challenge homophobic and biphobic bullying they must also reflect on their own practices and attitudes in order to assess whether they are subtly reinforcing this prejudice on a daily basis. We return to this later.

KEY POINTS

✓ Schools may be the only place where children and young people are having prejudiced views challenged.

✓ Homophobia can be enforced through our collective subtle behaviours and innuendo that communicate powerful messages to lesbian, gay, bisexual and heterosexual young people.

✓ We cannot challenge homophobia or biphobia without challenging all the assumptions about gender which inform this behaviour.

✓ Silence can send the loudest message about the value placed on lesbian, gay and bisexual identities.

CHAPTER 5

What Is the Impact on those Being Bullied?

Homophobic and biphobic bullying can affect a pupil's emotional and social wellbeing and their physical health. They are likely to remove themselves from social interactions in class and other activities they previously enjoyed. You are likely to witness their seemingly inexplicable slump in grades and whole-day or 'in-school' truancy. They are 'there' but not attending all their lessons in order to avoid their tormentors and even if in class physically they are definitely not 'there' in terms of concentrating on the lesson. Ultimately you may observe their departure from your school early or a move to a different school. The severity of the effects on a pupil depends entirely on the individual, their resilience and coping strategies. Inconveniently for teachers, different pupils are unlikely to respond to homophobic or biphobic bullying in the same way. We and the schools in which we work however have a legal, ethical and moral obligation to provide equal access to education and equal protection under the law for all pupils.

For many pupils worried about matters of sexuality, schools are unsafe and survival – not education – is the priority. (Weiler, 2003, p.10)

Box 5.1: Homophobic and biphobic bullying in the UK
Youth Chances (METRO Youth Chances, 2016) is a social research project aiming to identify the needs of lesbian, gay, bisexual, transgender and questioning young people. Led by the charity METRO, the Youth Chances project conducted online survey of 7000 young people aged 16–25 about their experiences of education,

employment, health services, relationships and sexuality. The survey found that:

- three in four LGBT young people have experienced name-calling

- one in two LGBT young people has experienced harassment and threats

- one in four LGBT young people has experienced physical assault

- two in three LGBT young people felt their school supported its pupils badly in terms of sexual orientation and gender identity issues.

These negative experiences proved to have a devastating impact on the mental health and wellbeing of LGBT young people with:

- 52 per cent of respondents reporting having engaged in self-harm

- 42 per cent seeking medical help for anxiety or depression

- 44 per cent reporting thoughts of suicide.

(METRO Youth Chances, 2016)

National surveys such as those conducted by METRO's Youth Chances project in the UK (Box 5.1) frequently indicate that homophobic and biphobic bullying is prevalent in schools. Teachers do not always recognise the homophobic bullying that occurs however and pupils do not always report the homophobic or biphobic nature of the bullying they experience. Many lesbian, gay or bisexual pupils have few opportunities to acquire coping strategies or learn how to be resilient in the face of such bullying or name-calling. Bullying can cause severe and lasting damage in adulthood to the self-esteem, wellbeing, happiness and potential of those who must endure it as a young person.

To gain an accurate snapshot of attitudes towards and experiences of homophobic and biphobic bullying in your own school it is useful to conduct an attitude survey to secure a broad understanding of your pupils' experiences. This does not have to be solely about homophobic or biphobic bullying but can capture pupils' views about all forms of prejudice-based bullying. By undertaking an attitude survey you will be able to identify how homophobic, biphobic, disablist, transphobic, racist or sexist bullying manifests itself, the impact it has on your pupils and where these problems cross over. It may highlight, for example, that biphobic bullying is prevalent among pupils online yet they do not know how to report or respond to it. Gaining an insight into the experiences of your pupils will allow you to direct resources to address areas of need.

When I was at school and during my years in teaching, pupils who experienced homophobic or biphobic bullying too often left at 16 years of age, exiting with qualifications much lower than their potential would have allowed them in happier circumstances. There is an historic link between bullying and low educational achievement. It is therefore logical to assume that the prevalence of homophobic and biphobic bullying results in lesbian, gay and bisexual pupils being especially disadvantaged when it comes to educational attainment. Such pupils however frequently cite physical sports as the most feared activity within school but consider the library and study areas to be sites of refuge (Monk, 2011). This complicates the often taken-for-granted assumption that lesbian, gay and bisexual pupils are failing to fulfil their academic potential.

When lesbian, gay and bisexual pupils do go on to attend university it would be interesting to know which subjects they study and whether their academic choices are limited by their experiences at school. Little research has explored this to date. Further exploration into the experiences of lesbian, gay and bisexual people at university and in the workplace may continue to confirm what has for too long been the case – that in commerce and industry lesbian, gay and bisexual people (particularly gay men) are more than likely to be 'in' at work compared with their peers in the service industry or arts. For example, there are disproportionately far higher numbers of 'out' lesbian women in our police service and armed forces than there are 'out' gay men.

To explore with any thoroughness the connection between sexual orientation and educational attainment would be impossible without also addressing issues of gender, socio-economic background, disability and race. The point here is that when young people are homophobically or biphobically bullied it can impact on them in varying ways (see Box 5.2) and low academic achievement is not the only signifier of distress. A school where any bullying is tolerated creates an unsafe learning and teaching environment for all.

Box 5.2: Types of responses to homophobic or biphobic bullying

When young people are homophobically or biphobically bullied, they can respond in a number of ways:

- Deny their sexuality either to themselves (if lesbian, gay or bisexual) or others who make reference to it.

- Develop low self-esteem and a negative self-image, lose self-confidence and limit their own aspirations.

- Project resentment onto other open or 'obvious' lesbian, gay or bisexual young people.

- Demonstrate feelings of anger (towards self and others), defensiveness, passive-aggression, shame or moroseness.

- Display self-ridicule to gain social acceptance (known as pro-behaviour).

- Adopt risk-taking behaviours online and offline.

- Practise self-harm or ideate suicide.

- Distrust others, leading to isolation, loneliness, suspicion or paranoia.

- Experience changes in sleep patterns, appetite or health – reported by parents or pupils.

- Display changes in attitude towards school and schooling, including truanting from school or certain lessons.

Bullying feeds into a wider school culture of negativity which, as a visitor, one can perceive quite palpably. A school's governing body – regardless of whether the school is a local authority run state school, an academy, a free school or an independent boarding school – is subject to the government's demands that schools make themselves safe places for each pupil: which means being safe from bullying.

Although it is the school governors' legal responsibility to ensure this is happening, it is the leadership team's ethical responsibility to effect this. It is important that all staff, at all levels, are aware of the school's approach to addressing every form of bullying.

A life lived out of authenticity – in which lies are told to others (and even oneself) about who one 'is' – is both emotionally exhausting and obstructive to any young person's, or indeed adult's, emotional and even physical development. Homophobia and biphobia have negative effects on the health and wellbeing of young people and those around them. They may internalise it as they negotiate their own identities at school. Self-confidence can be severely undermined with homophobia or biphobia directed inwards and manifesting as self-loathing.

Too many lesbian, gay or bisexual young people report feeling any number of negative emotions: anxious, stressed, worthless, ashamed, angry, isolated and fearful with feelings of incredible loneliness and a sense of abnormality. These emotions can lead to depression, self-harm, eating disorders, alcohol or drug dependency or suicide attempts. It is well recognised that suicide and suicide attempts are far more frequent in those young people who identify as lesbian, gay or bisexual than in the general youth population. The role of homophobic and biphobic bullying in contributing to these negative emotions and mental health issues cannot be underestimated. As Box 5.3 highlights, the connections between being bullied and suicide have been evidenced across the world.

Box 5.3: Bullying and suicide

Suicide is the leading cause of mortality in people under 35 in the UK. DitchTheLabel (2018) conducted a study into bullying that explored its prevalence and the impact it has on those targeted, perpetrators and witnesses. The study also explored levels of suicidal ideation among those affected. The studies indicated that:

- bullying affected 22 per cent of children

- 34 per cent of those targeted had experienced suicidal thoughts

- individuals perpetuating homophobic or biphobic bullying also have an increased risk of suicidal behaviours

- 56 per cent of those who had been both perpetrator and target had experienced suicidal ideation.

Box 5.4: ChildLine and bullying

In 2018/19 the UK counselling charity ChildLine delivered 573 counselling sessions about homophobic, biphobic or transphobic bullying.

School is where many of these young people experienced such bullying. Young people expressed to ChildLine how unbearable school life could be. Bullying was contributing to them having panic attacks, low self-esteem, concentration issues, skipping lessons, running out of school and poor attendance. Young people were often very concerned about how this was affecting their overall academic performance and mental wellbeing.

Some young people told ChildLine that they felt there was a lack of understanding and support at school around LGBT issues and that interventions concerning bullying were ineffective. At some schools however, there has been a positive change in the level of support being offered and young people told ChildLine about the impact this has had.

From what young people tell ChildLine it appears that many are going through their sexuality issues alone. Young people felt that nobody understood what they were going through and when they tried to express how they were feeling they often experienced negative reactions from family members and/or bullying from peers.

ChildLine considers bullying a significant issue and one that can seriously affect the mental health and wellbeing of those subjected to it. The charity recommends that talking about sexuality and raising awareness in schools can help increase young people's understanding and reduce bullying.

From ChildLine's work, it is clear that greater awareness, education and support should be more accessible in schools for both young people and the significant people in their lives.

ChildLine Information Service (personal communication, 2019)

Recognising oneself as lesbian, gay or bisexual can manifest itself in a number of ways. Similarly, coming out can follow a variety of permutations. Some people go into flat denial and attempt to fit in with their peers by dating the opposite gender to 'prove' they are heterosexual. Others are aggressively homophobic or biphobic in order to distance themselves from 'accusations of gayness'. Most lesbian, gay or bisexual young people however come out either to a trusted friend, a favourite teacher, a youth worker (or similar), a sibling or, not uncommonly, a grandparent. This often takes a great deal of thought and reflection because there is the possibility of losing close friends and being disowned by family. The latter is a horrifying prospect for almost all young people.

Most older lesbian, gay or bisexual adults have grown up believing that their sexuality is something of which to be ashamed and that in many circumstances they must hide it. The younger the adult, the less likely they are to feel this except where religion or culture confer powerful early messages about same-sex relationships in a negative way. While much older lesbian, gay or bisexual people will have heard themselves and others referred to directly and indirectly as queers, fairies, poofters, dykes and the like they are less likely to have heard insults in the classroom. There was a time when, although derided, a gay, lesbian or bisexual person was sneered at in spiteful lowered tones as 'one of them' but the issue was not one heard in their classroom. Today's generation of young people however are the ones to be aware of their sexual orientation and arguably the most well adjusted to it. Ironically it is also the generation to have heard 'That's so gay!' most frequently deployed as a put-down, insult or derogatory remark. Whenever 'gay' is used inappropriately it means variously pathetic, dull, rubbish, unfashionable, idiotic, ridiculous, stupid, uncool, boring, broken, ridiculous, naff, crazy and so on. It is vital to acknowledge here that each adjective is a deleterious one conveying a powerful sense that whatever it is being applied to is without value or worth: undesirable, less-than, objectionable or negative.

There are myriad reasons why lesbian, gay and bisexual people, now in their 40s or older, did not come out while at school. Most were fearful of censure, rejection and, for some, violence from classmates or family members. Some cultures are incredibly and actively hostile towards lesbian, gay and bisexual people and their relationships. The pressure on young people who live in these cultures to marry someone of the opposite gender is huge. It is true that some do not even realise they are lesbian, gay or bisexual thanks to a lack of positive role models and the portrayal of heterosexuality as 'the norm' created by television, films, books and advertising. This is particularly true for many black, Asian and other minority ethnic young people.

It is actually quite surprising how many people have the courage not to marry someone of the opposite gender such is the pressure on us all to do so. From the time we first kiss someone of the opposite gender aged four, in a playground or at a children's party our parents, grandparents and friends of parents are delighted and often proceed to reinforce the absolute 'when you grow up and get married' at any given opportunity.

Today, Britain is a nation of mostly secular, white British people for whom religion does not exert much influence on whether a young lesbian, gay or bisexual person decides to come out and later go on to marry someone of the same gender. Many other people however feel obliged to marry someone of the opposite gender despite knowing full well they are incompatible. There is research to be undertaken to establish how lesbian women who have married men negotiate their predicament but some gay men who marry women go on to have clandestine sexual assignations with other men facilitated by apps on their smartphone, surreptitiously visit public sex environments (woodlands or public conveniences) or live an isolated life, out of authenticity, where their sexuality and therefore true identity is soul-destroyingly subjugated. It is certainly true that many more divorced men and women are going on to enter gay and lesbian relationships than ever before while more people whose spouses have died are entering such relationships similarly. Some leave their spouse when their children leave home.

Identifying publicly as lesbian, gay or bisexual can be a very traumatic experience for anyone regardless of social class, age or the level of support from family. For a sizeable minority staying in the closet feels safer than risking social and workplace ostracism. Coming out as lesbian, gay or bisexual at school can mean having precious few people to turn to for advice and help when it is needed.

Whether lesbian, gay or bisexual pupils are out or 'in' they may feel a sense of guilt. Everyone, whether we care to admit it or not, has a deep-seated desire to be 'approved of'. Lesbian, gay and bisexual young people long to be accepted for who they are and are too often at risk of searching everywhere to find that acceptance. If they are 'in the closet' they experience a variety of emotions. Closeted youngsters may feel guilty for not being honest with their families, their friends and themselves. Not having anyone to turn to for guidance and advice can be a debilitating and very lonely experience. That feeling of aloneness is why lesbian, gay and bisexual young people may make unsafe decisions and risk-take often into and throughout adulthood.

One of the issues with which EACH and other training providers has always grappled is negotiating a course between the need to illustrate to adults (with responsibility to support young people who come out) why homophobic and biphobic bullying must be challenged, on the one hand, and not being seen to pathologise gay young people by over-emphasising the negatives of being young and lesbian, gay or bisexual on the other. Agencies, research findings or individuals who shroud-wave, constantly portraying gay young people's existence in terms of mental health issues and pathologising their experience of coming out do no one any favours.

Homophobia and biphobia will only end when society catches up with the laws we have passed to protect lesbian, gay and bisexual people and create safe and equal places of work and study. Then we can stop placing emphasis on what goes wrong for gay young people (and subsequently adults) when we fail to meet their needs.

Society is predominantly heterosexual and lesbian, gay and bisexual people are reminded of this fact on a daily basis. In recent years, it has been heartening to see an increase in representation of gay, lesbian and bisexual people in advertising. Lloyds Bank ran a television commercial featuring an older gay couple getting engaged with the strapline 'He said yes!' (Duffy, 2016). The much-anticipated annual selection of Christmas adverts has, for the past few years, frequently included lesbian and gay couples. Sainsbury's and Tesco have both featured families with lesbian and gay parents involved in the usual festive capers (Pink News, 2017; McCormick, 2016). Samsung, while advertising a new phone, has featured a lesbian couple expecting a baby (Samsung, 2019). What is affirming is how companies such as these are targeting the public with advertisements that a brand manager, even ten years ago, was unlikely to have commissioned. Meanwhile countless companies regularly run visible campaigns celebrating LGBT equality during Pride month. At its most simple this often takes the form of changing the company logo to a rainbow flag but other companies run large-scale campaigns featuring LGBT people – for example, Uber's 2019 campaign 'The Many Voices of Pride'.

These are indeed welcome and positive moves compared with flies in the ointment such as Katy Perry evidently considering it okay to release a single entitled 'Ur so gay' in 2008 (Perry, 2008) and Alan

Carr's (PETA, 2014) questionable stance when criticised for urging us all to 'Be a Little Fairy for Animals' on behalf of PETA (People for the Ethical Treatment of Animals) and subsequently describing those who were offended by the commercial as 'Oh, so worthy gays. The most homophobia I get is from gays #selfloathing' (Carr, 2014).

KEY POINTS

✓ Gay, lesbian and bisexual pupils are often offered few opportunities to acquire coping strategies or learn how to be resilient in the face of homophobic bullying or name-calling.

✓ Homophobic and biphobic bullying can affect a pupil's emotional and social wellbeing and their physical health.

✓ Coming out takes a great deal of thought and reflection because there is the possibility of losing close friends and being disowned by family.

✓ A life lived out of authenticity – in which lies are told to others (and even oneself) about who one 'is' – is emotionally exhausting and obstructive to emotional and physical development.

✓ The hostility demonstrated towards lesbian, gay and bisexual people by some cultures cannot be underestimated.

CHAPTER 6

How to Respond: Practical Advice

In this chapter three fundamentals are covered. First, how we should respond to verbal and physical homophobic and biphobic bullying. Second, what reporting mechanisms can and should be put in place to prevent it in the future, and third, what sanctions and celebrations of achievement regarding this bullying should look like.

Although we often hear the criminal justice system referring to its adoption of a 'zero-tolerance' approach towards certain crimes and schools in the UK ran with this in the 1990s and throughout the noughties, it should be acknowledged today that adopting a similar approach to any kind of bullying without putting measures in place to help pupils understand why it is entirely unacceptable will ultimately fail. Not every child *will* simply 'get over' someone in their class coming out as lesbian, gay or bisexual.

Responding to incidents of homophobic or biphobic bullying should go hand in hand with prevention. Where bullying behaviours are predicated on prejudiced views it is vital your school engages critically with these attitudes and takes action to deal with both the behaviour and the attitudes underpinning them. Further guidance on preventing homophobic and biphobic bullying can be found in Chapter 9.

Your school must make it clear to your pupils that homophobic comments are as serious as racist comments and homophobic or biphobic bullying as serious as other forms. Your school must respond consistently and effectively to incidents. This will indicate to those reporting that they are taken seriously and encourage their reporting while discouraging perpetrators.

There's a lot of stuff going on that teachers choose to ignore. It all depends on how the teacher is feeling that day because one day it could be fine and the next day Hell's gates could open and you don't know what's going on. The bullying can be too much to deal with or too little to concern them and they just ignore it. And that happens a bit and you think if nobody is going to help, what's the point in asking for it. (Brooke, 15)

Your school will already have procedures in place to respond to incidents of bullying and these procedures should be applied to incidents of homophobic and biphobic bullying. Procedures need to:

- de-escalate and stop its persistence

- protect the pupil(s) experiencing it

- hold to account the pupil(s) perpetrating it in a reasonable, proportionate and consistent way

- apply relevant sanctions to the pupil(s) involved and ensure they learn from the incident

- restore, as far as possible, good relationships between pupils.

Part of these procedures will include helping pupils understand why homophobic and biphobic bullying is unacceptable. This will mean having age-appropriate dialogue with year or tutor groups about lesbian, gay and bisexual people their rights in society and laws affecting the pupils once they enter the world of work and wider society in general.

CASE STUDY: Sir Bernard Lovell Academy, South Gloucestershire

We always bring staff back to the school's agreed-on definition of bullying which is: an imbalance in power repeated over time between one personal group and another personal group. Students are encouraged (by their tutor and house officers) to report bullying via student services or they can tell the safeguarding team or any adult regardless of why they are being bullied.

PROCEDURE

- First incident: tutors asked to talk to aggressor and target (this is normally enough to stop the bullying).

- Second incident: now recorded as bullying, tutor logs on to CPOMS (Child Protection Online Monitoring and Safeguarding system) (as homophobic/biphobic bullying) and behaviour team/house team take control, parents are informed.

- Two-week and four-week check-in with target and perpetrator.

- If the bullying continues, then punishment: day in isolation, temporary exclusion, permanent exclusion.

We have separate behavioural, safeguarding and pastoral teams. These teams meet every day after school to discuss the day's events. We always have a member of the special educational needs team present. This is important because often a pupil's needs will require input from some or all of the teams. The Principal attends in cases where we need to discuss exclusions.

Our aim is to 'educate first rather than punish first'. We explain LGBT terminology to the pupils and have an LGBT+ group that meets once a week. We also have a mentor scheme and can offer counselling sessions if needed.

Our culture tries to encourage staff to be that 'go to' person, to 'step up'. If a pupil comes to you, they trust you. Every adult in the school needs to be child focused. When they step into the building every day they should be available to the children and hold them in 'unconditional positive regard'.

Any school looking to challenge homophobic or biphobic bullying should get its anti-bullying policies right, its processes right, its structure set up and its staff trained to enable it to happen. Then when any kind of bullying – including homophobic bullying – happens people know what to do. You treat homophobic bullying the same as other forms of bullying.

Greg Lyle, Academy Safeguarding Lead, Sir Bernard Lovell Academy, South Gloucestershire

Responding to verbal incidents

Staff should feel able to discuss issues of homophobic and biphobic bullying with pupils, parents and deal with incidents quickly and effectively before situations escalate. Phrases such as 'That's so gay!' and homophobic language are often used without consideration and it is too frequently ignored because teachers have not been taught how and why they should respond and still too many lack the confidence to challenge homophobia and biphobia if they recognise it.

Homophobic language in schools has to be challenged because not only is it a micro-aggression in and of itself but also ignoring it propagates a culture of homophobia and biphobia and bullying will surely follow. This language should be challenged within a general programme of work the school undertakes in challenging the problem of homophobic bullying and negative attitudes towards lesbian, gay and bisexual people. This is not a singular response to the difficulties that arise. Any action to challenge homophobic language should be taken within the framework of the school's behaviour policy. Staff cannot and will not intervene effectively and consistently if it is not part of the school's policies and procedures.

Casual homophobic language is common in schools but if it is not challenged pupils will think that homophobia is acceptable and they will leave school remaining steadfast to this view. This is when they will come unstuck: either in the workplace or the street where homophobia and biphobia will not be tolerated by co-workers or members of society going about their everyday lives. The police will recognise reported incidents as 'hate crime', an offence punishable by law. It is therefore important to challenge homophobic language whenever it occurs in our schools.

If you hear a pupil use homophobic language you should intervene appropriately explaining that it is unacceptable, offensive and a form of discrimination. Boxes 6.1 and 6.2 provide practical guidance on how to intervene, whether you are in a primary or secondary school. It may seem time consuming at first to challenge a pupil every time you hear the phrase 'That's so gay!' Eventually however pupils will tire of being challenged. If this is coupled with effective prevention initiatives pupils will not only recognise that they are not allowed to use this language in school but also begin to understand *why* it is unacceptable and even challenge the language themselves.

Of course, some pupils will take more time to understand the importance of this issue. They will need to understand the sanctions that will apply if they continue to use this language. If it remains a repeat issue you may want to consider the school's hierarchy of sanctions. Further information about working with those who bully is available in Chapter 7.

Box 6.1: Responding to verbal incidents in primary school

Primary school pupils may not understand that their comments are inappropriate. When you hear a pupil use homophobic language you should consider the following points when dealing with the situation:

- Do they understand the word that has been used and its meaning?

- Do they understand the difference between heterosexual people and lesbian, gay or bisexual people?

- Are there any motivating factors concerning the pupil's behaviour? For example, are they targeting someone who has a lesbian, gay or bisexual parent or does not behave like a 'typical' boy or girl?

- Do they realise that the comment was inappropriate and hurtful?

- Do they understand the difference between appropriate uses of the word gay, for example, and inappropriate uses?

- Have they apologised for their behaviour and to the individual they were targeting?

Box 6.2: Responding to verbal incidents in secondary school

Pupils in secondary school are more likely to have an awareness of lesbian, gay and bisexual people and for their comments to be based on actual prejudice or ignorance. If you hear a secondary school pupil use homophobic language you should consider the following when dealing with the situation:

- Does the pupil understand that they have been homophobic or biphobic?

- Are they targeting someone who is lesbian, gay or bisexual, or perceived to be? Do they understand that they are treating the pupil differently because they think or know that they are lesbian, gay or bisexual?

- If the pupil is targeting someone who is perceived to be lesbian, gay or bisexual, do not confirm or deny these 'accusations'. The sexual orientation of the target is irrelevant to the issue which is that the perpetrator is being homophobic or biphobic. Affirm the target's right to come to an understanding of their own sexual orientation on their terms.

- Has the pupil considered the effect that their language and behaviour is having on the target?

- Does the pupil acknowledge that what they are doing is bullying and understand it in the context of prejudice?

- Does the pupil understand the hierarchy of sanctions which apply to engaging in homophobic or biphobic bullying?

- Has the pupil considered how they might change their behaviour in the future?

Responding to physical incidents

Pupils may be reluctant to report any bullying incident because they fear that staff will assume they are lesbian, gay or bisexual possibly disapprove and be in a race to tell their parents.

More often than not [those targeted] can feel discouraged from saying anything because they feel shame or don't want to make things worse because that is the traditional route that safeguarding can go. It can make things worse so people just keep quiet. (Max, 16)

Physical bullying immediately indicates that a young person is at risk and the school's overarching strategies implemented to safeguard pupils could very well be required here, involving the school's child protection officer, agencies such as EACH and possibly the police if the physical harm constitutes a crime. Homophobic and biphobic violence can quite easily be a crime and schools' anti-bullying policies should be rigorously enforced and regularly updated to keep pupils safe from physical harm.

Physical abuse can include hitting, punching or kicking (see Table 1.1 in Chapter 1 for a comprehensive illustration). Young people also report that they experience being threatened with a weapon or receiving death threats.

Homophobic or biphobic physical abuse can also include sexual abuse. Some young lesbian women report that they have experienced sexual abuse and humiliation from both heterosexual girls and boys. Other young people who are lesbian, bisexual or gay feel under pressure to engage in sexual activity with someone of the same gender to 'prove' that they 'really are gay'. Some also feel pressured into engaging in sexual activity with someone of the other gender to 'prove' they are not lesbian or gay. Bisexual people may face pressure to engage in sexual acts with people of both genders. These pressures can be heightened by physical abuse and pressure from peers. Physical and sexual abuse is a definite indication that staff will need to take steps to safeguard a pupil. Further guidance about dealing with disclosures is available in Chapter 8.

Physical homophobic and biphobic bullying can affect anyone regardless of whether or not they are lesbian, gay or bisexual and has to be challenged and stopped within a school.

Primary school pupils can experience both verbal and physical homophobic and biphobic bullying motivated by the fact that a child seems 'different' from their peers and teachers should recognise this and intervene. Challenging homophobic and biphobic bullying must start in our primary schools if we are to end and prevent it in our secondary schools.

All staff members should regularly refresh their awareness of their school's anti-bullying policy and its 'hierarchy of sanctions' when responding to homophobic bullying. When intervening in a physical incident it may be possible to follow the same lines of enquiry as employed when intervening in verbal incidents. Any incident of physical bullying however will need to be coupled with an appropriate sanction even if it is an isolated incident. If the issue is ongoing, in necessary circumstances the school will need to consider permanent exclusion (see Box 6.3).

Box 6.3: Guidance for exclusions

The Department for Education's guidance on exclusions (2017a) states that a decision to exclude a pupil should be taken only:

- in response to serious breaches of the school's behaviour policy

- if allowing the pupil to remain in school would seriously harm the education or welfare of the pupil or others in the school.

Only the headteacher in charge of a pupil referral unit (or, in the absence of the Head or teacher in charge, the most senior teacher who is acting in that role) can exclude a pupil.

In cases where a headteacher has permanently excluded a pupil for persistent and defiant misbehaviour, including bullying (which would include racist or homophobic bullying), or repeated possession or use of an illegal drug on school premises, the Secretary of State would not normally expect the governing body or an independent appeal panel to reinstate the pupil.

Dealing with homophobic and biphobic bullying consistently

All staff should be consistent in indicating that homophobic comments are unacceptable and ensure that pupils targeted by them feel supported. Staff need to be sensitive when talking to pupils about incidents taking into account the concerns or worries the pupil may have. This is addressed in Chapter 8.

If a pupil uses homophobic language, all members of staff must point out the effect their language is having on other people, stressing that phrases such as 'That's so gay' are not harmless banter but part of homophobia whether the pupil appreciates this or not. All staff must be signed up to this too.

Monitoring and recording homophobic and biphobic bullying incidents

Most schools have mechanisms for recording incidents of bullying. Monitoring incidents enables a school to identify patterns of behaviour and the extent of the behaviour and then take proactive steps to challenge it. It is best practice for schools to record all incidents of bullying (and acknowledge its different forms), including homophobic and biphobic bullying. Schools that use monitoring processes are able to modify their bullying policies to respond to specific trends and issues. Incorporating incidents of homophobic and biphobic bullying into these existing systems and sharing this information among staff is an invaluable means of raising awareness about the issue among everyone.

It is important that recording procedures are detailed and comprehensive enough to allow for effective analysis. If information about what should be recorded and how is not clearly outlined to staff the quality and detail of recording can vary enormously. Without sufficient and detailed data bullying incidents cannot be robustly scrutinised and patterns may be missed. In addition to recording the particulars of incidents, monitoring procedures should also keep a record of the action taken, by whom and when, along with an indication of any follow-ups undertaken to ensure the intervention was effective. By recording the actions taken in response to reported and recorded incidents schools are in a stronger position to investigate whether these interventions were successful and change their approach if necessary.

CASE STUDY: Yeo Moor Primary School

Speaking out is very much to do with culture and relationships. You can have structures like worry boxes and if you ever fail to monitor them or keep them safe then there are some real problems. Something that does work is being around – walking around at lunchtime, being in places where children can access you. Having a designated non-teaching member of staff in charge of pastoral care is great for this and we walk around at lunchtimes and sit with the children. To make this work you have to have established the understanding that you actively enjoy talking with children and are keen to listen and do small talk about pets or whatever. Part of our mantra is that it is about relationships and you can go a step further by saying that the quality of interaction is important: people speaking nicely to each other. This is too simple to be called a strategy but I believe it is hugely important. Just saying a nice sincere 'Hello' in the morning is a building block to enabling a child to speak out about something that worries them.

Roland Lovatt, Headteacher, Yeo Moor Primary School, North Somerset

An effective anti-bullying log should include:

- a clear definition of bullying, including prejudice-based bullying, so staff are clear on what they need to record

- a detailed account of the incident, including where and when it took place who was involved including target, perpetrator and any bystanders, the nature of the incident and whether it was prejudice based (homophobic, biphobic, sexist, transphobic, racist, disablist, etc.)

- actions to be taken, by whom and by when.

Not all incidents of homophobic and biphobic bullying will be reported to teachers and staff. Pupils may lack confidence in bullying interventions and fear the repercussions of admitting they are a target of homophobia. Therefore be sure to include questions about homophobic bullying on anonymous pupil surveys in your own school or authority.

Evaluating progress also makes it easy to celebrate success and helps those involved keep focused and motivated. Schools should evaluate progress every term, reporting back to all stakeholders, especially pupils. This will help show progress as well as what is remaining to be done.

Sanctions

A school should establish how its range of sanctions can be applied most appropriately to the varying severity of homophobic and biphobic bullying. A mapping exercise can be used as a professional development and discussion tool with all staff and governors to develop a shared understanding and consistency of practice in applying sanctions to those who perpetrate homophobic or biphobic bullying. Participants are given a series of, preferably actual, scenarios of homophobic and biphobic bullying, or wider descriptive statements, and then asked to map them against the school sanctions framework (see Box 6.4).

Box 6.4: Homophobic bullying scenarios

Jenny, 13
Jenny has been experiencing homophobic bullying for several months. A group of girls in her year have spread rumours about her sexual orientation, exclude her from activities and call her 'the lezzer'. Jenny has reported the incident to her tutor and asked for help.

Ahmed, 15
Ahmed reports that there is homophobic graffiti written about him in the toilet and that he knows who wrote it.

Rachel, Amy and Jess, 16
Amy and Jess have recently started a romantic relationship. Although Amy has been out as a lesbian for a year, Jess has only recently told

her friends that she is bisexual. Rachel feels left out when the two girls spend all their time together and don't invite her. She starts spreading rumours that Jess is sleeping around and the relationship with Amy is just an experiment. This upsets both Amy and Jess and they stop talking to Rachel, leaving her isolated from her friends.

Joe, 14
Joe has recently come out on Facebook as gay. Many of his Facebook friends wrote homophobic and nasty comments on his Facebook wall. Joe told his mum who reported it to the school.

Ryan and Lee, 6
Ryan and Lee are in the playground playing tag. When Lee trips over and begins crying, a teacher overhears Ryan call him a 'gay boy'.

Responding to incidents of homophobic and biphobic bullying should acknowledge the 'hierarchy of sanctions' which the school set out for responding to inappropriate behaviour. This helps staff respond effectively to bullying. The sanctions should be developed in consultation with pupils and informed by their views. When determining sanctions, it is helpful to consider the following questions adapted from the Welsh Government's (2011) guidance on homophobic bullying:

- What sanctions should apply if a pupil uses homophobic language such as 'That's so gay!' unintentionally and it is not directed towards anyone?

- How can sanctions be used when homophobic language is directed at an individual or group, for example, 'You're so gay!'?

- How will sanctions escalate if the bullying behaviour is continual?

- Should sanctions be different if the pupil targeted by homophobic or biphobic bullying is not lesbian, gay or bisexual?

- How should sanctions be used if a pupil is targeted because their friend, parent or other family member is lesbian, gay or bisexual?

- What strategies can you employ to deal with a group who are bullying an individual?

- If a pupil is gay but does not want their parents to know how will you keep parents informed of the bullying they are experiencing?

- Could EACH or another training provider assist the school, the target(s), the perpetrator(s) or their families?

Sanctions should also be visible and well publicised within school to pupils, parents, staff and governors. It is important that all stakeholders are aware of the consequences of homophobic and biphobic bullying, their rights and responsibilities and the sanctions they may experience should they engage in this prejudice-based bullying.

Celebrating success

While no one wants to have to apply sanctions (because it indicates unacceptable behaviour has been exacted), we know that there are times when they must be implemented. What so many schools forget to do is celebrate achievements and success in challenging bullying (including homophobic and biphobic bullying). Celebration elevates achievements around anti-bullying work to be shared by the whole school and fosters a culture of positiveness and an affirmative school ethos. Celebrating success helps to assure pupils, staff, governors and parents that the school is taking meaningful, effective steps to improve policy and practice.

Here are some of the ways in which your school can celebrate successes concerning homophobic and biphobic bullying:

- Demonstrate in assemblies the role of mentors or nominated members of staff (in secondary schools) or playground buddies (in primary schools) in challenging homophobic and biphobic bullying. Explain why it is vital never to be a bystander or to collude in others' bullying.

- Use the outcomes of a review by pupils and staff of your school's anti-bullying policy as a way to engage the whole school in recognising what is already being done and what still must be done.

- Use a range of national and locally validated schemes to celebrate achievements in challenging bullying.

- Schools in a partnership or federation may opt to run a joint conference on, for example, human rights or equalities issues and focus on prejudice-based bullying or harassment. This could examine school, local, national and international issues. Remember to invite local agencies to input into this such as your local council's equalities team lead.

CASE STUDY: Churchill Academy & Sixth Form, North Somerset

In addition to setting up Libra, the group providing student leadership on LGBT+ issues within the school, we have introduced the 'Pot of Gold' awards where students can nominate staff who have gone out of their way to demonstrate inclusive practice or to make sure that students are aware of LGBT issues within or beyond the curriculum. Pot of Gold at the end of the rainbow...the students came up with that!

Chris Hildrew, Headteacher, Churchill Academy & Sixth Form, North Somerset

KEY POINTS

✓ Responding to incidents should go hand in hand with prevention.

✓ All staff should be consistent in indicating that homophobic and biphobic bullying is unacceptable and ensure that pupils who experience it feel supported.

✓ Responding to incidents of homophobic and biphobic bullying should recognise the 'hierarchy of sanctions' which a school has developed for responding to inappropriate behaviour.

✓ Monitoring incidents enables you to identify patterns of behaviour, the extent of the bullying and to take proactive steps to challenge it.

✓ Celebrating successful anti-bullying work elevates its achievements and fosters a positive culture.

CHAPTER 7

Working With Those Who Bully

We know that bullying is unwanted, aggressive behaviour which involves a real or perceived power imbalance. The behaviour is repeated, or has the potential to be, over time. Both young people who are bullied and those who bully can experience lasting mental health issues.

> People are more likely to listen to a pupil who's really popular than a teacher. (Ellis, 14)

Working with those who bully homophobically or biphobically is challenging as it is often perpetrated by the most powerful pupils who command other pupils' attention, and even that of their teachers, either by being 'popular' with pupils, teachers or both or through being 'a force to be reckoned with'. These pupils are not, in truth, lastingly 'popular' but they are influential. We know that in bullying there is an imbalance of power, sometimes achieved through physical strength and sometimes attained by manipulation (using access to information to humiliate, harm or control others). Bear in mind that power imbalances can change over time and in different situations, even if the same people are involved.

Perhaps you have witnessed cases where pupils consider their bullying behaviour justified and regularly witness how parents attempt to justify their child's bullying if either the child or the parents are challenged. It is not uncommon for pupils who bully to experience a home life where there is scant positive, caring adult attention, where discipline is inconsistent and 'binary' (proffering too much privilege countered with punitive sanctions for misdemeanours) with some parents being either emotionally or physically aggressive, or both. It is hard for such children to develop empathy or sympathy and they regularly fail to make cause-and-effect links between their actions and consequences. Rather than reflect on their behaviour when punished for bullying others they will resent adults in authority or their peers whom they have bullied. Where sanctions for bullying are largely absent or inconsistent young people who enjoy the power and social status gained from it are very unlikely to change. Without supervision, clear expectations and consistent consequences, this is practically a given.

When responding to an incident of homophobic or biphobic bullying you should consider how your response can alter the behaviour and attitudes of the perpetrator along with any bystanders who may support or reinforce the perpetrator's actions. As outlined in Chapter 4, homophobic and biphobic bullying are underpinned by a range of attitudes, values and beliefs. It is important we understand the perpetrator's motivations for targeting someone homophobically or biphobically before deciding on the action to take. You and others who work with children in a professional capacity play a vital role in changing the behaviour of those who bully. For interventions and responses to be effective you need a clear understanding of the roots of bullying behaviour and a confidence in your school's strategies. It is equally important to realise what approaches can inadvertently make the bullying worse.

When considering the root of the bullying behaviour the following questions can help:

- Does your pupil understand that homophobic and biphobic bullying are not acceptable in their school?

- Do they understand why?

- Does your pupil understand the impact their actions have had on the pupil experiencing the bullying? Do they recognise what they have done?

- Does your pupil think their actions are justified?

- Does your pupil understand that homophobic language is unacceptable however inadvertently used: 'Oh man, that is SO gay!'?

Pupils cannot be expected to learn by themselves that homophobic and biphobic bullying is unacceptable. If they do not know why they need to be told. Pupils who have not been taught previously that homophobic or biphobic bullying is wrong will take time to realise that their behaviour is inappropriate. In the short term, any incident of bullying needs to be dealt with by employing the appropriate sanctions as agreed in your school policy. Someone not prevented from bullying or made to see the absolute inappropriateness of their actions will rarely stop bullying. Continuation of bullying will:

- promote a group culture where causing harm by bullying is seen as acceptable and everyone tacitly accepts collusion with bullying as the norm

- demonstrate that the school either condones the behaviour and attitudes which underlie it, seems powerless to prevent it or does not care

- in many cases, lead a young person to become an adult who causes harm to others by engaging in anti-social, harassing and potentially criminal behaviour.

Any time an incident of homophobic or biphobic bullying occurs your school must respond and demonstrate that this behaviour is not condoned. A strategic approach to sanctions and interventions is explored in Chapter 6. Your school's anti-bullying policy and staff training should clearly cover the agreed procedure for responding to a bullying incident, including the sanctions, reporting procedures and whether the pupil's parents should be informed. The pupil must acknowledge the harm they have caused and why the actions are in breach of school policy. To encourage pupils to think about the consequences of their actions consider these points:

- Does your pupil recognise that action needs to be taken to make the bullied pupil feel better? Does your pupil accept responsibility? It is crucial they understand that they must take responsibility for making the situation better. They should be urged to generate suggestions concerning next steps and recognise that the bullied person will have their own views.

- Will your pupil make assurances that they will not bully someone again? Do they understand that the incident cannot be repeated? The pupil must understand that the key to resolving the incident is a commitment not to reoffend. They must appreciate the importance of a general change in their behaviour.

- Does your pupil understand what other sanctions will apply if they continue to bully? Are they clear about the escalation process and how this can ultimately end in exclusion? Pupils should not be discouraged from expressing their views but they need to understand the difference between expressing an opinion and being insulting.

Ignorance

Building on points made above, if pupils do not fully understand why homophobic or biphobic bullying is wrong when sanctioned or punished, instead of reflecting on their own behaviour, they are likely to blame authority figures or peers whom they have distressed. This can lead to ramifications or the problem escalating for the target.

Responding to one-off incidents of homophobic or biphobic bullying can only go so far and to truly eradicate the problem a longer-term strategy needs to be implemented. Pupils who bully often have a negative view of school and its role. School culture cannot be underestimated for its role in fostering bullying. Make use of curriculum opportunities, work in partnership with pupils, parents and governors to develop policies and ensure everyone knows in advance and accepts the sanctions that will be applied if pupils fail to follow the rules. Ultimately, only dialogue and discussion about sexuality held in a positive, constructive arena will change your school's culture. This will not happen if the topic is only ever discussed in direct connection with homophobic or biphobic bullying. Further guidance on how to implement this long-term strategy is detailed in Chapters 9 and 10.

Behavioural problems

It's the [pupils] with behaviour issues or those that don't behave well in class. Maybe they didn't have much teaching on this growing up and they don't understand it. (Lilah, 13)

For some pupils, bullying and other forms of social aggression are more related to impulsiveness and poor social skills than to an effort to control others. When this is true, cognitive-behavioural interventions to improve impulse control and structured social skills training may also be helpful. Anger management strategies may be effective with these pupils, although these are unlikely to help a pupil whose aggression is planned and executed with pre-meditation.

Bullying can also be a response to emotional distress or mental health issues. Too often this is overlooked and little attention is paid to the emotional wellbeing and mental health of those who bully. The UK government has issued specific guidance on mental health and behaviour in schools to help teachers better identify underlying mental health problems in pupils and prevent them from being wrongly labelled as troublemakers (Department for Education, 2018). Promoting positive mental health should go hand in hand with work around behaviour and bullying.

There are a number of approaches which may be considered to stop bullying. One might believe that those who bully have low self-esteem and need work to build this up. Aggressive pupils can, in actual fact, have very high self-esteem: their aggression emanating from a sense of privilege and entitlement (invariably imbued in them by their parents). It is rarely effective to employ counselling strategies based on building self-esteem with an aggressive child.

You might wish to consider peer mediation. Mediation-based strategies are based on compromise rather than blame. When carried out by young or relatively untrained mediators however mediation in bullying situations risks solidifying the power differential between the young person who bullies and the bullied young person.

Effective interventions with a pupil who bullies often involve strategies such as reality therapy or cognitive-behaviour therapies which make them accountable for their actions and for the impact of those actions on themselves and others. Work with family systems and consultation and advocacy with schools is also often necessary. As William Glasser (1975) wrote in *Reality Therapy*, '[In therapy] someone cares enough about the patient to make him face a truth he has spent his life trying to avoid: he is responsible for his own behaviour' (p.27).

Effective interventions are built on the following principles adapted from the US Department of Health and Human Services guidance (2011):

- Have in place a contingency for unexpected outcomes along a continuum starting from non-hostile to escalating and increasingly damaging consequences. The aim is to make the perpetrator recognise the cost of their bullying behaviour and guide them to consider alternative behaviour.

- Hold to account for their actions the pupil who bullies. Confront excuses that minimise the behaviour ('It was just a bit of banter') or externalise the cause of the behaviour ('He was acting gay so I hit him'). Ensure that the pupil fully acknowledges their behaviour. Emphasise that they had other options and that no matter what the provocation only they are fully responsible for their decision to bully.

- Support parents and colleagues in holding their children or pupils to account for their actions and not to allow rationalisations ('She only gets into mischief because she's so bright and isn't challenged enough academically').

- Once your pupil is able to recognise significant problems with their behaviour, mental health professionals can work with them to establish goals for improvement. The pupil's progress can be monitored and tracked. The pupil can have this reflected back at them as they demonstrate improvements and develop a sense of pride in what they are achieving. If we work with the pupil on specifics such as asking them to identify precisely what they hoped to achieve by a particular bullying behaviour we can work towards finding other ways to gain a sense of reward that is not connected to subjugating someone else to make the child doing the bullying feel better about themselves. A lot of this revolves around dealing with anger management issues in the child. If you can get to the root of why they are angry you are already half way to making their bullying stop.

- Assist the pupil in building better relations with their family members and school mentors.

- Support parents and siblings to both acknowledge and endorse improved behaviour in their family member, affirming non-aggressive ways of behaving with child-relevant rewards.

- Nurture genuinely felt emotions such as empathy and sympathy to help your pupil understand and recognise the ramifications of their behaviour. It is important, however, that we do not maintain this 'learning' at purely a cognitive level. If we do this there is the chance that we help our pupil to get even better at bullying. Once they understand what hurts people they can get even better at doing it!

- Develop your pupil's sense of 'conscience'. Once they recognise how their bullying behaviour has caused them to be sanctioned or punished they can begin to appreciate the effect of their actions on their targets.

Pupils who believe their actions are justified

Some pupils will believe that their homophobic or biphobic behaviour is justified and this can often be reinforced by parents. Even if pupils and parents have certain religious or moral views about lesbian, gay and bisexual people this does not mean that bullying people should be in any way tolerated. It will be helpful to consider the questions below when dealing with a pupil who feels that their homophobic or biphobic behaviour is justified:

- Are you and your school colleagues confident to raise or respond to issues of sexual orientation even when your pupils express challenging or disconcerting opinions? Do all your pupils recognise the difference between a committed viewpoint, intransigence and bigotry?

- Have your school's pupils and parents had it explained explicitly that homophobic and biphobic bullying will not be tolerated and why and how their personal view of lesbian, gay and bisexual people can be at odds with the school's stance on challenging bullying? Does everyone connected to the school understand the difference?

- Are both pupils and parents aware of your school's policies relevant to homophobic and biphobic bullying? Do they understand that any negative behaviour manifested by their child could well have serious ramifications?

- Do your pupils and parents appreciate that sanctions are in place regarding bullying and that these plus accordant punishments will be applied equally regarding homophobic and biphobic bullying?

Pupils should not be discouraged from expressing their views concerning lesbian, gay and bisexual people and related issues but they should be taught the difference between expressing an opinion and self-consciously being derogatory. Both pupils and parents must understand that their personal views (including religious ones) can never justify bullying.

Parents need to appreciate the severity of homophobic and biphobic bullying and understand what sanctions will apply if they are to help prevent bullying. They should be made aware that, in the UK, schools have a legal duty to respond to and prevent homophobic bullying in accordance with the Equality Act 2010, Public Sector Equality Duty 2011 and Education and Inspections Act 2006.

If parents are considered a significant factor in the child's behaviour and are unwilling to engage voluntarily with either the school or the local authority it may be appropriate to consider a parenting order. A parenting order is a civil court order which consists of two elements:

- A requirement on the parent to attend counselling or guidance sessions (e.g. parenting education or parenting support classes) where they will receive help and support to enable them to improve their child's behaviour or attendance – this is the core of the parenting order and lasts for three months.

- A requirement on the parent to comply with such requirements as are determined necessary by the court for improving their child's behaviour or attendance at school. This element can last up to 12 months.

Homophobic language

Many schools will be indicating consistently that homophobic and biphobic bullying is wrong and pupils will recognise that it is unacceptable to treat someone differently because they are lesbian, gay or bisexual or are thought to be. Where schools often struggle is with the use of homophobic language and phrases such as 'That's so gay' or the increasing use of the word 'faggot'. In these cases, pupils will often not see that their actions have a direct consequence for anyone. As a result, it will often be perceived as 'harmless banter'. When so much legislative progress has been made for lesbian, gay and bisexual equality pupils might question whether co-opting the word 'gay' as an insult really matters. Language changes all the time and many young people will argue that calling their homework gay has nothing to do with their opinions on same-sex relationships. In fact, sometimes young people who identify as lesbian, gay or bisexual will themselves use 'That's so gay' in this context. For these pupils the word can have several meanings which they think have no connection to their attitudes towards themselves and other lesbian, gay or bisexual people. There is also a chance pro-behaviour is at play here. This is when someone who is conscious of feeling 'outside' society's 'mainstream' deploys (usually self-deprecating) humour to divert attention away from their, for example, disability, ethnicity or sexuality. It sometimes works but is more often counterproductive.

The structured prompts adapted from East Sussex and Brighton Hove PSHE Advisory Team (2002) are useful practical tips for dealing with homophobic language (see Box 7.1). They provide staff with a variety of simple responses: each operating at a varying degree of remove from the situation.

Box 7.1: Structured prompts for homophobic language

Dismissive response:

'I'm not prepared to listen to language like that.'

'I really don't want to have to hear remarks such as this.'

Interrogative response:

'What makes you say that?'

'What did you mean by that?'

'Shall we talk about why people think like this?'

Didactic response:

'Language like that is unacceptable.'

'We have a rule in school about the use of homophobic language.'

Personal response:

'I'm not happy with what you've said.'

'I find that language really offensive.'

'What you've said really disturbs me.'

Institutional response:

'Our school doesn't tolerate language like that.'

'A lot of people would find that remark really offensive.'

East Sussex and Brighton Hove PSHE Advisory Team, 2002

To punish pupils for using homophobic language without discussion can however propagate its use and fail to engage with the real experiences of young people. To assume homophobic or biphobic attitudes without listening to young people's views is to pre-judge and censor them. The problem here is that beyond causal calling of homework 'gay', these young people have few opportunities to express their attitudes around sexuality constructively. We must never allow young people to brush us or their peers off with, 'But I didn't mean anything by it', and staff dealing with the inappropriate use of homophobic language need to feel confident when responding to it. Allowing homophobic language to go unchallenged will only appear to reinforce its acceptability in our classrooms, corridors and playgrounds. Challenging homophobic name-calling and bullying should be combined with opportunities to explore and reflect on pupils' experiences, values and knowledge to ensure they understand the impact of their actions. Staff need to feel safe and confident in addressing homophobia and biphobia and in most schools' professional input is going to be required from a nationally recognised and qualified agency such as EACH.

Engaging the local community

Schools will be aware of the range of views and attitudes regarding issues of sexuality and many will be educating pupils who come from backgrounds where there exist divergent and conflicting views on this. Some individuals or sections of society may question or reject the principles of equality but every school is required by law to uphold these principles. Discussing bullying is a great place to begin engaging your pupils with these sensitive issues and your school will need to make use of a full range of strategies when working to engage with parents, families and communities including the following:

- Communicating your school's position on all forms of bullying and clearly naming homophobic and biphobic bullying in all your relevant policies.

- Using every means available to keep your parents informed about your school's stance on issues of bullying: your school prospectus, newsletters, website, social media platforms, digital message boards, homework diaries and a myriad of communications available to your school office.

- Ensuring your parents know how they can report and seek help concerning homophobic and biphobic bullying.

- Offering tailored support to parents who need this either because their child is experiencing bullying or due to their child's bullying behaviour.

- Utilising the formal mechanisms already in place for parental engagement, including the use of parenting contracts or home-school agreements. A lot of parents are only too pleased to receive your school's help!

If you do not feel that any of the above is currently robust enough in your school raise this with your manager or the senior leadership team as appropriate.

A strategic approach to applying sanctions and interventions

Your school needs to establish how the range of sanctions available to it can be applied most appropriately to different incidents of homophobic and biphobic bullying. As mentioned in Chapter 6, a mapping exercise can be used as a professional development and discussion tool with all staff and governors to develop a shared understanding and consistency of practice in applying sanctions to those who participate in homophobic and biphobic bullying. Participants are given a series of scenarios of homophobic and biphobic bullying or wider descriptive statements and are then asked to map them against the school sanctions framework.

Implementing permanent exclusions and involving the police

Homophobic or biphobic behaviour in your school may involve criminal offences such as assault, theft, criminal damage, harassment, misuse of communications, prejudice-based crime (hate crime) or sexual offences. Where bullying is particularly serious or persistent it will be necessary (either to protect the person experiencing the bullying or respond appropriately to an incident) to implement exclusions (temporary or permanent) or involve the police in dealing with criminal offences which have been committed. Your school's senior management team will need to follow the procedures they have put in place for involving the police in cases of this nature.

KEY POINTS

✓ Pupils will rarely if ever change their homophobic or biphobic bullying behaviour if they are not brought to an understanding of why – from inadvertent use of 'That's so gay' to violence – it is never acceptable.

✓ Pupils with additional needs will need a bespoke approach to help them understand why homophobic and biphobic name-calling and bullying are wrong.

✓ Where incidents can be managed in school this is always the best policy. Involving the police should only be a last resort but in certain circumstances will be unavoidable.

✓ Consult everyone concerning your approach to challenging homophobic and biphobic bullying. You will achieve far greater buy-in from parents if the governors and teachers have devised your school's approach with your parents and pupils and then published it on your website.

✓ While making the school's tier of sanctions crystal clear be sure to celebrate milestones reflecting achievements and strides the whole school has made in reducing all incidents of bullying.

CHAPTER 8

Sensitive Handling
of Disclosures

There will always be the expectation that teachers will respond empathetically or at least sympathetically to a pupil disclosing that they have been a target of bullying but when that bullying is homophobic or biphobic in nature it is particularly important to be sensitive to a pupil's situation and needs. Remember, bullying is bullying regardless of a member of staff's religious, cultural or personal convictions. Every pupil has a right to be protected from it and you have a duty of care towards each child in your charge.

In fact, pupils may be reluctant to speak to members of staff precisely because they feel sensitive issues will have to be shared widely and all school staff should be aware of how to handle pupil disclosures of a personal nature. Most lesbian, gay or bisexual pupils who do not experience homophobic or biphobic bullying are unlikely to find the need to come out to a teacher. It may be known that some pupils are gay across the school if, for example, they are or have been in visible relationships with other pupils. Most lesbian, gay and bisexual pupils will only be out to their friends or a close-knit network.

Learning a pupil is gay either because they or their friends tell you is not necessarily a disclosure. It is often just a simple statement of fact about their lives. It is important in these moments to still offer affirmation and support but not undue concern. After all, pupils being comfortably out as lesbian, gay or bisexual in your school is a positive sign and testament to your school's inclusive ethos. If you were to learn that a heterosexual pupil fancied a classmate it would not see you reaching for the crisis pamphlets or calling home unless you had reasonable cause for concern. The same judgement should be applied when supporting lesbian, gay and bisexual pupils.

Even if there is a visible lesbian, gay and bisexual student body within your school such as an LGBT group there will likely be pupils who are not out or are unsure of their sexual orientation. Partially down to the lack of existence of 'out' positive role models within a school, pupils can still fear homophobic or biphobic discrimination particularly if they do not have access to a supportive network of family and friends. These pupils may be more likely to become the target of rumour-mongering, gossip and more. Interestingly, pupils in schools EACH supports note that those who are 'suspected' of being lesbian, gay or bisexual are far more likely to be bullied than those who are openly so. Regardless of sexual orientation all pupils can perpetrate this kind of bullying behaviour particularly if they do not possess the emotional maturity to come to terms with others' sexual orientation. One should challenge any speculation about another pupil's sexuality highlighting that this too is unhelpful and affirm all pupils' right to come to an understanding of their identity on their own terms.

Often homophobic or biphobic bullying can result in pupils being 'outed' before they are ready. When you are the teacher faced with responding to a pupil's disclosure of homophobic or biphobic bullying it is likely you will be dealing with their coming out simultaneously. Of course, not all pupils who are homophobically or biphobically bullied are lesbian, gay or bisexual and not all lesbian, gay or bisexual pupils are homophobically or biphobically bullied. Yet even those heterosexual pupils who are targeted may find themselves questioning their sexual orientation as a result of homophobic or biphobic bullying. It is important that all permutations are dealt with sensitively and on the pupil's own terms.

Your school's confidentiality policy should provide a framework for staff when deciding whether or not they can offer confidentiality to a pupil who discloses information about themselves or their situation and this is explored in more detail below.

The reality is that a member of staff – whatever their role in the school – can offer only a degree of confidentiality. Where a member of staff is concerned that the pupil may be at risk of harm they must make contact with the school's safeguarding lead in order to discuss making a referral according to its procedures.

Staff should also be clear on distinguishing their own needs from those of the pupil. For example, if a pupil discloses themselves as lesbian, gay or bisexual the member of staff may need to look up further information or guidance on the issue in general as a response to a request from the young person. So long as no child protection issues present themselves during the course of your conversation your duty of care to the pupil is to preserve their confidentiality.

Health service staff operating a service on your school site (e.g. a school nurse) offer a slightly different degree of confidentiality although the principle of confidentiality is still limited according to whether or not the pupil is at risk.

> I used the internet to find out about me because [sexuality] wasn't talked about and I saw it as taboo. (CJ, 17)

As much as the internet offers pupils a window onto the world around them it does not educate them in the same way that a trusted adult can. The internet offers possibilities but it is not always safe and pupils need the support of adults to guide them through the usual storm and stress of young adulthood. Any lesbian, gay or bisexual pupil who needs our support but who goes without it will not thrive. At best they will switch off, coast through school and academically under-achieve. Too many however run the grave risk of becoming depressed (even if they do not recognise that they are) or turn to some form of self-harming behaviour (smoking, drinking, drug-taking, cutting or disordered eating) which occasionally does not manifest itself until adulthood or carries on into it.

A rite of passage enjoyed by the majority of heterosexual teenagers can so often be unavailable to the average lesbian, gay or bisexual teenager particularly those in rural areas or in families which maintain adherence to strictly heterosexual cultural activity. Outlets for sexual curiosity can then become internet chat rooms, pornography or geosocial websites. In all such places people may not be who they seem and a young person's subsequent introduction to such individuals and any sexual relationships can be dangerous, with fewer of the inherent safeguards and social pleasures enjoyed by heterosexual peers.

So, the next time you find yourself experiencing a 'doorknob moment' (someone telling you something really important and about which you should do something just as they have their hand on the doorknob and are poised to leave) it is not beyond the realms of possibility that one of your pupils is about to tell you that they are lesbian, gay or bisexual or that they are experiencing homophobic bullying or both. I say 'you' because you have picked up this book and you are interested in what it has to say. Someone in your school whom you would not seek out if you needed a friendly ear and reassuring words will not be sought out by your pupils either and in all likelihood unless they have been formally directed to will not read this book.

How can you be best prepared for such a disclosure by one of your pupils? Well of course you will be acutely aware that it will have taken them far longer to pluck up the courage to tell you than the time it takes to actually tell you. In fact, your pupil will have mulled over the issue for a very long time before deciding who to approach to discuss it. If they have chosen you it is because they have decided you are a trustworthy, empathetic person who will not judge them harshly but take what they have to say seriously. Good for you! Let us assume however that a pupil is yet to have done so and you wish to be prepared. The individual circumstances of coming out or disclosing homophobic or biphobic bullying will be specific to each pupil and accordingly require bespoke handling. It is possible nevertheless to adhere to the general principles detailed in Box 8.1.

Box 8.1: Handling disclosures of homophobic and biphobic bullying

1. Bear in mind you are as likely as not to be told about homophobic or biphobic bullying just as you are leaving for another lesson or about to have a really important meeting that has been postponed previously and which you really cannot put off again, or are eager to go to the lavatory which is not close by.

2. Factoring in point 1, it may be necessary to explain to your pupil that you absolutely want to listen to what they have to say and explain calmly and succinctly why at this moment you cannot. Be aware of your non-verbal communication as the pupil may hear one thing but misconstrue your body language: reading your need to be somewhere else as rejection. Above all, thank them for beginning the conversation and tell them you are looking forward to its continuance.

3. Arrange with them a time as close to now as possible when you can meet. In the interim, offer them someone who can listen to them right now (only if you know that you can), for example

your school counsellor, nurse or similar, and listen to whether this is what they want.

4. When you meet, do so in a calm, safe space where you know you will not be interrupted by telephones or other people. Ask them to tell you what is on their mind.

5. Let the pupil get out their opening sentence(s). Prior to any confidential conversation, you may have outline your child protection responsibilities (see 'Confidentiality' in this chapter). Your pupil may go on to disclose information that you consider harmful (to themselves or others) and this you are legally obliged to act on. You need to be clear and transparent about the legislative responsibilities you have regarding disclosures you consider harmful to the pupil. Inform them of the circumstances in which information may need to be shared, with whom and for what purpose. Overarchingly however ensure your pupil understands that, within the child protection parameters you have outlined, what they say will most definitely be treated confidentially

6. Listen to the rest of their story in a non-judgemental way.

7. If they are disclosing bullying encourage them to agree to the incident being formally logged through the school's system for recording bullying incidents and explain that this can be anonymised.

8. Ask them what they would like you to do to help them.

9. Explain that they, or you on their behalf, may telephone EACH or another support agency to talk over homophobic or biphobic bullying should this be relevant to the pupil.

10. Thank them for talking to you (do not say 'confiding in' you).

Adapted from Save the Children (2008)

Pupils who have experienced homophobic or biphobic bullying may require immediate support following an incident but they may well also need ongoing support to feel safe in school. Targets of homophobic or biphobic bullying could need your support to tell their story fully and discuss how the incident has affected them. Reassure the pupil that ongoing support will be made available to them and that you will take action to prevent the same thing happening again to the best of your abilities. You have been honoured with being the recipient of your pupil's disclosure. Now you must honour this responsibility by helping them.

Sources of help to support you might include a colleague who arranges to meet with the pupil to 'check in' on how they are. You may feel that another member of staff is better placed to provide ongoing support than you and you need to explain to your pupil why this is the case and who this person will be. Are there dedicated pupils in the school (peer supporters or mentors) who could complement this role and with whom the pupil would feel safe and comfortable talking about either homophobic or biphobic bullying or coming-out issues? In some cases both the target of homophobic or biphobic bullying and its perpetrator (and respective family members) would benefit from specialist intervention. Consider inviting a training provider such as EACH to come to the school to provide targeted support for the pupil or training for the staff to help them support pupils in such situations in future.

In anticipation of a forthcoming meeting with a pupil who you think or know will be discussing either a disclosure around sexuality or telling you about homophobic or biphobic bullying it is worth bearing in mind these points:

- Lesbian, gay or bisexual issues are obviously not simply or just about sexual attraction and sex. There are deep emotions and wider relationships with friends and family to work through.

- Try to reassure your pupil that if they are lesbian, gay or bisexual they should feel no pressure to be 'out' and they should take things at a pace that feels comfortable for them.

- Encourage your pupil to think carefully about who, if anyone at this stage, they want to know that they are lesbian, gay or bisexual and why they do or do not want them to know.

- Ask your pupil to consider the reaction of those they will tell and any implications. If they are worried about ramifications, encourage them to reflect on how they will deal with situations which may arise.

- If they indicate any sense of shame or disgrace about being lesbian, gay or bisexual or being homophobically or biphobically bullied be positive and reassure them that there is nothing wrong with identifying as such. Positive affirmations and a supportive environment for gay pupils can help combat any internalised feelings of homophobia or biphobia which are so often borne out of negative depictions of lesbian, gay and bisexual people and the portrayal of heterosexuality as the only and 'normal' way to be.

- If a pupil discloses that they are questioning or are confused about their sexuality you can reassure them that this is a normal part of the process of developing and understanding their identity. Explain that in time they may identify as heterosexual, lesbian, gay or bisexual. Explore with them what these labels mean and their understanding of sexual orientation.

- If the pupil discloses that they are engaging in sexual activity or are considering having sex use your professional discretion to determine:

  - whether the young person is capable of understanding and consenting to the sexual activity in which they are or wish to be involved

  - the nature of the relationship between those involved particularly if there are age or power imbalances which may come within child protection concerns

  - if the pupil is adequately informed about safe sex and has access to appropriate advice

  - if the pupil is of the age of consent.

Disclosures of homophobic or biphobic bullying may include the disclosure of sexual bullying including potentially criminal acts such as sexual assault. Schools should therefore work to ensure that all staff are confident in their knowledge of its safeguarding referral processes.

If you are concerned that the young person may be at risk of sexual abuse or exploitation a referral should be made to your dedicated safeguarding or child protection officer or, if relevant, Child Exploitation and Online Protection (CEOP).

Confidentiality

Since 2000, when I began supporting teachers, youth workers and others who educate or support young people regarding coming out or homophobic bullying I have observed how unsure people are about where they stand on the issue of confidentiality.

As a basic rule, young people have the same right to privacy as adults. If a young person chooses to confide information about themselves this must remain confidential. You have legal responsibilities to pass on information to appropriate agencies if a young person discloses abuse or if not sharing the information would place a young person at risk of significant harm. A breach of confidentiality occurs when you share information of some sensitivity:

- without a justifiable reason for doing so

- without legitimate purpose

- without the permission of the person who provided it

- without the permission of the person to whom it relates.

Young people who disclose their sexual orientation or come out to you may not have done so to members of their family or to other staff members as they may deem the personal risk too high or expect discrimination or rejection. It is important to note that disclosure of sexual orientation is not a reason to breach a young person's confidentiality. If they also disclose information that places them at risk of significant harm their sexuality must still remain private until consent is obtained from the young person to share this information.

Consent must be informed. The person giving consent needs to understand why information needs to be shared, who will see or hear the information, for what purpose, and the implications of it being shared. Even in cases of disclosure of abuse it is best practice to inform your young person why this information is shared, with whom it is shared, and for what purpose.

You should not seek consent if to do so would place a young person at risk of significant harm, or place an adult at risk of significant harm, or would prejudice the prevention or detection of serious crime. It is still possible to share information for learning purposes among staff or in order to develop policy if the information shared does not enable the young person to be identified.

The key factors in disclosing information are as follows:

- Is there a legitimate purpose for you to share the information?

- Does the information enable a person to be identified?

- Is the information confidential?

- If the information is confidential do you have informed consent to share?

- If consent is refused, or there are good reasons not to seek consent to share confidential information, is there sufficient public interest to share information?

- If the decision is to share are you sharing the right information in the right way?

- Have you properly recorded your decision?

It is possible that either you or your colleagues will have little or no experience of having an openly lesbian, gay or bisexual pupil in the classroom. It will probably come as no surprise therefore that if your school is one where issues of sexual orientation equality and rights are rarely if ever discussed, and homophobia and biphobia are not actively challenged, very few young people will disclose their sexual orientation to any member of staff while at school.

Once homophobic and biphobic behaviour is challenged comprehensively and a more respectful culture established your school will need to address the following:

- Disclosures will increase. Pupils will choose to talk individually to teaching or support staff about the bullying behaviours they experience, witness, or even perpetrate and more generally about their lives and experiences which may involve coming out to you.

- Existing policies will need reviewing. The senior leadership team will need to revise your school's child protection and anti-bullying policies with staff, pupils and parents to accommodate issues related to coming out and homophobic and biphobic bullying.

- Recording systems will need reviewing. Your school's system for recording incidents is likely to need a new section for homophobic and biphobic bullying.

- Information may need updating. Your school probably will need to revise its list of external support agencies plus the range of statutory and voluntary agencies which offer complementary support services and training on issues related to prejudice-based bullying (see Appendix 5).

Parents

Finally, it is important to make reference to parents and their reaction when they learn either that their child has been the target of homophobic or biphobic bullying or that they have come out as lesbian, gay or bisexual. Parents are usually the adults in whom children feel most confident confiding but sometimes they feel they cannot because they are going to be rejected. This can have devastating results.

My parents use homophobic language all the time. (Syd, 13)

Many parents enter into a form of grieving process when they learn that their child is gay. Some parents recognise that their child is gay long before the child realises the fact themselves but others are shocked, bewildered, angry and only finally accepting of their child's sexuality. This is dependent on a number of factors including individual personalities, religious convictions and culture. Some parents never accept it and become estranged from their child. Some children choose to effect this estrangement themselves because of the degree of negativity shown by the parent. Some have no choice in the matter and are made homeless. The national charity the Albert Kennedy Trust exists to support young people in this situation.

KEY POINTS

✓ Reporting homophobic or biphobic bullying is not the same as coming out as lesbian, gay or bisexual but a pupil's disclosure of homophobic or biphobic bullying may be accompanied by their coming out.

✓ Lesbian, gay or bisexual pupils may be reluctant to report homophobic or biphobic bullying because they feel they may be 'outed' to their parents or the school before they are ready.

✓ If a pupil confides private information about themselves this must remain confidential unless they disclose abuse or not sharing the information would place the young person at risk of significant harm.

✓ Pupils who have experienced homophobic or biphobic bullying may require immediate support following an incident but they may well also need ongoing support to feel safe in school.

✓ Role models should not be drawn solely from sources such as television or music. Who are the lesbian, gay or bisexual positive role models in your school? Who are the heterosexual allies, particularly heterosexual men?

CHAPTER 9

Prevention

What do you see your school being 'for'? To teach children to pass examinations? To prepare them for the world of work? Or to ground them morally, ethically and socially as well as academically? Do your senior leadership colleagues and your governors share your vision for your school?

The fact is that not all of our pupils are having their educational needs met. Some are suffering because of homophobic or biphobic bullying and accordingly their schoolwork is paying a similar price. There will be a pupil or pupils leaving your school this academic year who did not thrive. They had a wretched time convinced that we were not there to help them. It is so easy to cater for the high-achieving pupils who not only reward us with the evidence of their intelligence or talent but can articulate so eloquently how we have helped them. The ones it is an effort to support demand more of us but not doing so means we 'lose' pupils – either actually because they leave the school or we lose their potential. They become frustrated and their parents too because despite all the responsibility and nurturing they invest at home they do not see this reflected in their child's schooling:

> I watched my handsome, witty, confident boy become ill with the constant abuse. He became physically ill and run down. He was mentally battered with continuous put-downs. He was very courageous to just set foot in that school day after day knowing what he would be facing but not even the very strongest could be expected to maintain any sort of self-worth under those circumstances. Eventually he calmly declared he would rather be dead than have to face that another day. (Clair, parent of a homophobically bullied 13-year-old)

It follows therefore that creating a positive and inclusive ethos where homophobic and biphobic bullying is recognised in all its forms, and pupils feel safe and confident to report such bullying, needs commitment throughout the entire school (see Figure 9.1). It requires everyone to purposefully promote the equality of lesbian, gay and bisexual people as part of a school ethos that celebrates diversity and challenges all forms of inequality.

The answer to challenging homophobic and biphobic bullying is preventing it in the first place. At the heart of prevention must be a positive school ethos where pupils and staff treat one another with respect because they know this is the right way to behave. This positive ethos must be promoted as soon as anyone joins your school and walks through its gates.

Your school may be engaging in good practice in relation to celebrating diversity and challenging inequality on the grounds of race, faith, gender or disability but the legacy of the UK's Section 28 of the Local Government Act 1988 has historically stifled the encouragement of lesbian, gay and bisexual equality in school. Despite this, recognising this equality does not require reinventing the wheel. Schools with an established ethos of celebrating diversity and promoting equality of any kind will already have the mechanisms in place to begin celebrating lesbian, gay and bisexual equality. Building a positive and inclusive school culture demands a combination of committed senior leadership, effective school policies, robust staff training, targeted initiatives and inclusive curriculum opportunities.

If it is LGBT History Month or another calendar date related to LGBT matters please bear in mind that it is not enough simply to rainbow wash your school's logo to show this recognition without putting in place considered activities reflecting its commitment to the issues and engagement with your pupils at a fundamental level to demonstrate that it is safe for them to speak about anything that may be on their mind. Be prepared too to effect changes as a result, be these curricular, policy related or practical.

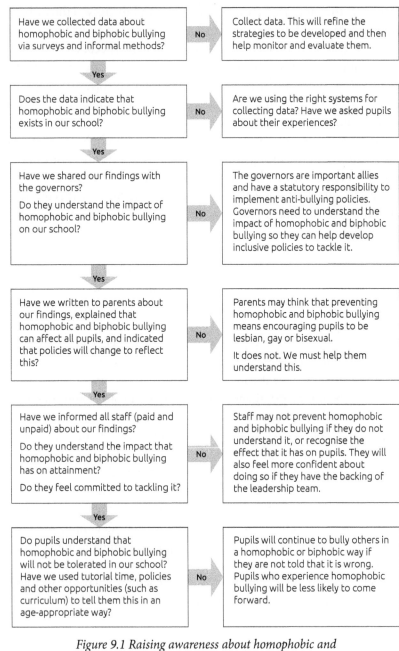

Figure 9.1 Raising awareness about homophobic and biphobic bullying in school (EACH, 2014)

Senior leadership

Securing the support of senior members of staff such as your headteacher and the governors is essential to ensuring that a positive and inclusive culture is reflected in a school's day-to-day work. Not only are senior leaders responsible for developing policies and procedures in line with government guidance and legislation they should also ensure that such developments are undertaken in collaboration with pupils, parents, staff and governors.

On top of this, senior leaders should support the professional development of staff by ensuring that everyone understands the policies and procedures in place and has access to appropriate training. As employers, they are also responsible for ensuring that staff are not discriminated against on the grounds of sexual orientation. Therefore, headteachers and governors have a duty both to ensure that staff are able to challenge homophobic and biphobic bullying and feel protected from it too.

School policies

Developing a set of inclusive policies helps to ensure that your school's values are communicated clearly as well as understood and enacted by all members of your school (see Figure 9.2). Pertinent policies are ones relating to behaviour, anti-bullying, equal opportunities, safeguarding, e-safety, staffing and school improvement. Such policies should be working documents which communicate expectations to the whole school. Once again, any changes to policies should be conducted in consultation with pupils, parents and staff.

It is important to remember that bullying will never be eradicated in schools if policies which are both consulted on and 'owned' by the entire school are not put into practice.

Teachers are far less likely to challenge inappropriate behaviour in their pupils if policies are absent, inadequate, 'unplugged' or the only move towards a whole-school approach to challenging homophobic bullying amounts to an ad hoc assembly and sticking up a poster telling pupils to 'get over' people being lesbian, gay or bisexual.

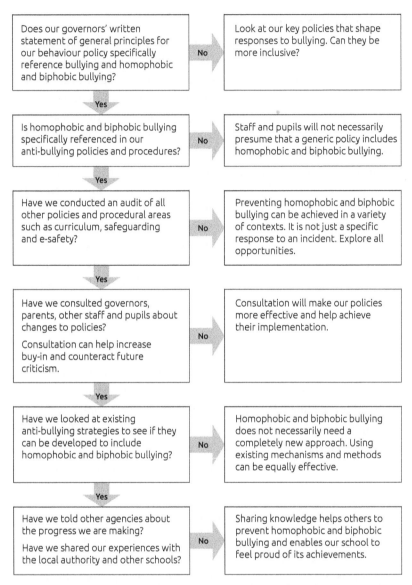

Figure 9.2 Developing policies, practices and procedures (EACH, 2014)

CASE STUDY: Churchill Academy & Sixth Form, North Somerset

The unique thing about Churchill's approach to LGBT issues is most definitely the students. We have a number of very brave young people who understand their ability to make a difference to others by being role models and trailblazers. Lots of our discussions in Libra centre around this and it was during one of these in fact that [two pupils] offered to give an assembly.

On top of this I would say that Churchill's core principles – kindness, curiosity and determination – are integral to an inclusive learning environment. Teachers and students do genuinely use these concepts to guide their teaching and learning. It's through these that we all learn to be accepting of others and of ourselves. The idea of support to be better through enlightenment is something that encompasses all three and I believe our Libra students are willing to do this (as well as report incidences of bullying and nastiness) when peers make a mistake or are unkind.

Rachel Lowrie, Key Stage 3 Leader of Learning for English

Policies should make explicit reference to homophobic bullying alongside other forms of prejudice-based bullying and behaviours. They should also recognise that this form of bullying can happen online as well as offline. Linking policies also helps create a clear and consistent message and demonstrates that bullying is part of a 'continuum of behaviour' rather than something separate (Ofsted, 2012, p.13). Further information about developing your school's anti-bullying policy can be found in Chapter 10.

Staff training

Anti-bullying measures are most effective when every staff member understands the principles and purpose of the school's policy, its legal responsibilities regarding bullying, how to resolve problems and where to seek support (see Figure 9.3). Staff training therefore has a vital role to play in preventing homophobic and biphobic bullying. It is important that staff develop an understanding of how prejudice-based bullying differs from general bullying so that they acquire the skills to respond to and challenge the underlying prejudices.

Understanding the terminology is helpful because it allows you to frame the conversation informed by knowing how somebody identifies as, for instance, gay or bi. (Ellis, 14)

It may be helpful to check that your staff understand and feel comfortable using terminology such as heterosexual, lesbian, gay and bisexual. Staff training should not only ensure that your colleagues can respond to the prejudiced-based behaviour of others but prompt them to reflect too on their own attitudes and role in reinforcing or shaping the possible prejudices of pupils. Staff can play a crucial role in perpetuating homophobic and biphobic bullying, either by harbouring their own prejudices or failing to challenge homophobic or biphobic behaviour. This should never be underestimated. Staff training should not start and end with teachers. It is important to also include learning mentors, teaching assistants, lunchtime supervisors, site managers and administrative staff. All staff should understand school policies and their responsibility for upholding and modelling a positive and inclusive school culture.

CASE STUDY: Bradley Stoke Community School – Good As You

At Bradley Stoke Community School we felt that having EACH work with us on delivering training on homophobic and biphobic bullying to staff was a key factor in ensuring that everyone thought about their personal responsibility as part of the bigger whole-school picture. The training was met with overwhelmingly positive feedback and staff were motivated and inspired to establish a consistent approach to tackling homophobic language use. As a school, we agreed that doing this in a non-confrontational way which challenged inappropriate language while seeking to inform and educate was a preferred route. The staff team felt empowered to work together and were clear that any persistent issues would need a more consequence-based approach. What was particularly interesting was that students had a really broad range of views about how they wanted the school to tackle issues of inappropriate language use. These ranged from detentions and exclusion to the death penalty! It was clearly a very emotive topic and the student voice was very strongly telling us that they wanted us to take action where it was needed.

We instigated a 'Good As You' focus week. We took the word 'gay' and created staff t-shirts adding the slogan 'Good As You'. The majority of staff wore these for the entire focus week and it caused a great deal of interest among students. To back up this message, all assemblies for this week focused on the results of their anonymous survey and challenged student attitudes to the words they sometimes used. This approach was very successful. Conversations between staff and students showed that we were making an impact and making them think about the words they were using. For us however this wasn't just about having a focus week, it was about starting to build the foundations where young people feel safe and secure to simply be themselves.

We see this work as just the beginning and have already started making plans for our next phase, which aims to develop a staff and student equal opportunities forum – a champion group for all students who may feel 'different' because of their background, sexual orientation, ethnicity or religion. We have planned to ask EACH to support us with this by providing training for student volunteers who can act as mentors to other young people in school and we will be exploring the use of technology to support students who may find face-to-face conversations difficult.

As a school, we thread positive attitudes about celebrating difference, tolerance and diversity throughout the curriculum and in everything we do as a staff team. Our work in making sure that students feel confident that other students will not bully or intimidate them because they are a young gay, lesbian, bisexual or transgender student is part of a continuing journey for us and we are grateful for the continued support from EACH.

Susie Beresford-Wylie, Director of Student Support and Olympus Academy Trust Safeguarding Lead, Bradley Stoke Community School, South Gloucestershire

Teachers and wider school staff play a number of roles throughout the school day and move between them imperceptibly and continuously, for example educator, nurse, warden, counsellor, parent, confidante, custodian and advocate. This is especially noticeable where positive role models are absent from a pupil's home life. Teachers can often be the only source of comfort and security to lesbian, gay or bisexual pupils and it should never be underestimated what value they place on the psychological and physical refuge provided by a caring, interested teacher, learning support assistant, school counsellor or mentor. Memories of and gratitude towards such adults remain with a person their entire life. Unfortunately, not every school offers such support and pupils continue to feel anxious and very alone.

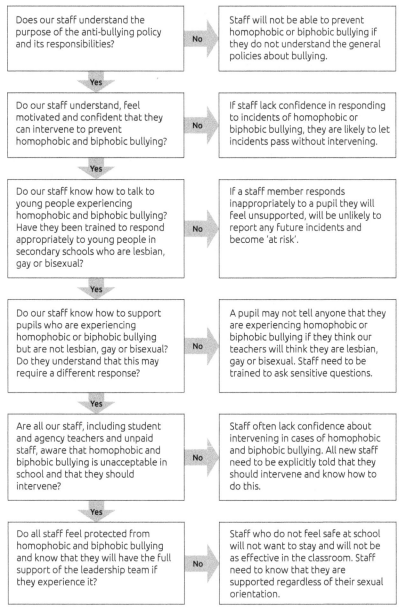

Figure 9.3 Steps for staff development (EACH, 2014)

Targeted initiatives

Targeted initiatives provide an opportunity to reinforce a positive and inclusive school culture. This can include awareness days, workshops, signposting and drop-in sessions as well as involving the wider neighbourhood and utilising a variety of organisations. Various calendar opportunities exist throughout the year for these initiatives such as Anti-Bullying Week (coordinated by the Anti-Bullying Alliance), Safer Internet Day, LGBT History Month in February, Bisexual Awareness Week in September and the International Day Against Homophobia and Transphobia (IDAHOT) on 17 May every year.

CASE STUDY: Bristol Brunel Academy

We started with a lunchtime group that welcomed LGBT+ students and allies. Through working with EACH we have been able to train staff and find out from our young people how we could improve ourselves as an inclusive setting. We supported each tutor group across Years 7–11 (ages 12–16) to engage with a month-long scheme of work that culminated in students contributing a Pride pledge for our Pride Wall. We also had a cake sale to celebrate Pride where cakes, badges and stickers were handed out and greatly received. Last year we had a non-school-uniform day to celebrate Pride which will become an annual event for the school. This combination of the day-to-day and special occasions has had a huge impact on the atmosphere around the building and is regularly commented on by staff, students and visitors.

Colin Clements, Inclusion and Safeguarding Lead

Schools do not have to be restricted to embarking on targeted initiatives within these months if it does not suit their programme. In fact, delimiting discussion of lesbian, gay and bisexual equality or discrimination issues (and particularly homophobic or biphobic bullying) solely to preordained calendar dates misses numerous opportunities for 'teachable moments' such as what is topical in the news. Members of staff with a connection to personal, social and health education or a pastorally related subject can similarly capitalise on topical and timely 'teachable moments' as they arise.

One example, for secondary schools, would be to explore the very recent trend exhibited by corporations such as banks, shops, train companies, legal and financial firms to 'rainbow' their logo with the Pride flag colours to signpost their support for UK Pride and its events. Much was made in the media in 2019 about whether retail and business organisations – or indeed pop stars – pledging their support for LGBT matters was as altruistic as this appeared. Is such a pledge sincere or useful PR to attract the confidence (and pound!) of lesbian, gay, bisexual and trans people? This is a valuable chance to address economic motivations for backing initiatives set against genuinely meant ethical support.

> When I went to Pride I was in the queue and overheard someone being homophobic. We were there to support LGBT people not insult them. It really annoyed me because they were just going there to party. They obviously weren't thinking about their surroundings. (Lilah, 13)

Sometimes pupils may present teachable moments from their own experience. Lilah's is an example of a teachable moment exploring what it means for heterosexual people to enter LGBT spaces without understanding the context. Similarly, in discussions about corporate Pride, this example is useful both for considering something that is topical and 'on trend' and the impact that being 'on trend' can have.

A topic for more experienced or confident teachers would be to explore the sentiments on both sides behind the protests in Birmingham to the 'No Outsiders' programme of LGBT inclusion which saw a group of protesters objecting to this programme outside primary schools. Much media attention was focused on this. This event creates a useful opportunity to look at the issue of religious sensitivities and LGBT matters and where priority is perceived to lie when opinions are set against the law concerning protected characteristics. (Protected characteristics are the nine groups protected under the Equality Act 2010: age, disability, gender reassignment, sex, sexual orientation, religion or belief, marriage and civil partnership, pregnancy and maternity, and race.)

Curriculum opportunities

> Assemblies and safety days make [learning about lesbian, gay and bisexual issues] an event [...] we should just have it fluidly throughout the whole curriculum instead of on certain days because that makes it feel separate to 'normal' school. (PJ, 16)

Raising awareness about issues of equality and diversity through the curriculum is key to preventing and challenging homophobic and biphobic bullying as it provides opportunities for pupils to understand, reflect on and challenge their own prejudice. The Wyedean School case study below describes the work of a school with whom EACH has worked since 2005 covering lesbian, gay and bisexual equality in its curriculum on a regular basis. Schools should make time in the curriculum to promote equal opportunities, enable pupils to challenge discrimination and stereotyping and introduce them to the concept that any kind of bullying is morally wrong and illegal in the workplace. It is also important that the curriculum meets the needs of its lesbian, gay or bisexual pupils. Schools should be mindful not to make assumptions about the sexual orientation of their pupils, families or staff in the delivery of lessons and ensure that all strands of diversity including sexuality are covered in lessons.

Subjects such as PSHE, citizenship, RSE or religious education provide good opportunities to explore equality and diversity. To truly embed a positive and inclusive culture there needs to be a strong emphasis on ensuring that pupils are able to extend and apply their learning to a range of subjects.

> The [LGB] curriculum is divorced from what's going on around us all. It needs to be rooted in the here and now and what's happening today and what has happened in history. Too much distance is put between the topic and lived experience. (Josie, 16)

Teachable moments in addition to those previously mentioned include challenging the use of the word 'gay' when used insultingly or disparagingly, and opening up a debate for instance about the Channel 4 video *Complaints Welcome* created to allow its presenters including Big Narstie, Rachel Riley, Kevin McCloud and Grayson Perry the chance to turn the public's complaints about them into a statement on their individuality. Another 'teachable moment' when exploring matters of equality includes looking at where in the world same-sex relationships remain outlawed as a way of exploring British values and colonial legacy. Pupils should have the opportunity to view lesbian, gay and bisexual equality and rights in the context of other movements such as those supporting equality for women, black, Asian and minority ethnic people and disabled people.

> We need to learn about history. We need to learn about oppression. (Syd, 13)

Pupils cannot be expected to understand how in the Republic of Ireland, for example, same-sex marriage was legalised in November 2015 while not legalised until four years later in Northern Ireland without exploring the historic and political reasons explaining this situation, set against other legislation around abortion, divorce and adoption.

Interviews with school children reveal time after time their exasperation that the legal history concerning sexuality is not explored when their school undertakes work on lesbian or gay matters, often with initiatives delivered in a vacuum with no historic context.

Schools should aim to use language which is gender neutral. Exploring with your pupils the etymology of words and how societal power is very much mixed in with our gendered vocabulary will be illuminating and fascinating to many pupils. Ask the girls why they are happy to be addressed as 'you guys' when part of a mixed-gender group while boys in a mixed group would baulk instantly at being referred to as 'gals' (while the girls would fall about laughing). Why are members of staff in schools referred to as 'Sir' when they are men while women are always 'Miss'? EACH works a school where female teachers are called 'Madam' to accurately reflect how an adult would address a woman with whose name they were unfamiliar or in a day-to-day context.

Masculine words, sports, pastimes and jobs continue to have greater status than feminine ones. You might want to discuss in PSHE, citizenship, history, English or modern foreign languages the implications of the feminisation of words ending in 'ette' (cigarette, statuette, leatherette): it reduces their status from the masculine and indicates a lower value or worth. You could similarly debate 'landlady' compared with 'landlord' or 'manageress' versus 'manager'. Two fantastic books on the sexism in the English language which have more than stood the test of time include *Boys Don't Cry: Boys and Sexism in Education* and *Language and Gender* (Askew and Ross, 1988; Goddard and Patterson, 2000).

CASE STUDY: Wyedean School LGBT week

During LGBT week at Wyedean School, Year 8 [aged 12–13 years] students have the opportunity to focus on a range of related topics that encourage them to consider the impact of prejudice both at school and in wider society. The week aims to raise the profile of the School's commitment to equality and make it an even greater community in which students can work and learn.

The Year 8 LGBT week engages younger students on these issues through lessons, assemblies and tutorials. During the week, subject teachers encourage reflection on a variety of related topics ranging from current attitudes towards same-sex relationships, a celebration of the ground-breaking contributions made to our society by LGBT people (for example Alan Turing) and the importance of language in our day-to-day conduct. The students also cover other important issues including attitudes to same-sex relationships and the terrible oppression suffered by LGBT people throughout history, as well as in countries around the world today. We also invite outside speakers including EACH to work with the students and staff, adding yet another dimension to the work. Wyedean School has worked with EACH since 2005.

It is great to see so many subjects and year groups getting involved to help raise awareness of our commitment to tackling homophobia and biphobia and the reasons for it. The response from the Year 8s is really encouraging and the students are very willing to share what they have learned from the lessons, tutorials and their work with EACH. Their comments demonstrate a growing understanding of the importance of homophobic language, the impact it can have and their role in challenging it.

Recent school surveys at Wyedean evidence a significant fall in the amount of homophobic language being heard. This has been down to the proactive work done by a great number of staff, students and outside agencies. One of the key reasons for the success of the project concerns the way in which staff have embraced it and this is in no small part down to EACH's training input at in-service training sessions, which puts our project's anti-homophobia and anti-biphobia drive firmly on the radar.

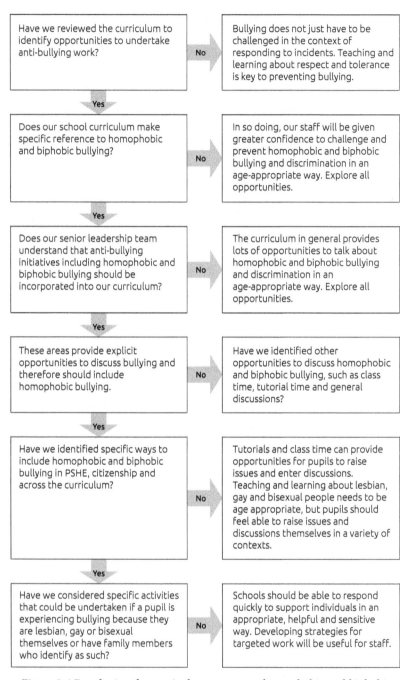

Have we reviewed the curriculum to identify opportunities to undertake anti-bullying work? → **No** → Bullying does not just have to be challenged in the context of responding to incidents. Teaching and learning about respect and tolerance is key to preventing bullying.

↓ **Yes**

Does our school curriculum make specific reference to homophobic and biphobic bullying? → **No** → In so doing, our staff will be given greater confidence to challenge and prevent homophobic and biphobic bullying and discrimination in an age-appropriate way. Explore all opportunities.

↓ **Yes**

Does our senior leadership team understand that anti-bullying initiatives including homophobic and biphobic bullying should be incorporated into our curriculum? → **No** → The curriculum in general provides lots of opportunities to talk about homophobic and biphobic bullying and discrimination in an age-appropriate way. Explore all opportunities.

↓ **Yes**

These areas provide explicit opportunities to discuss bullying and therefore should include homophobic bullying. → **No** → Have we identified other opportunities to discuss homophobic and biphobic bullying, such as class time, tutorial time and general discussions?

↓ **Yes**

Have we identified specific ways to include homophobic and biphobic bullying in PSHE, citizenship and across the curriculum? → **No** → Tutorials and class time can provide opportunities for pupils to raise issues and enter discussions. Teaching and learning about lesbian, gay and bisexual people needs to be age appropriate, but pupils should feel able to raise issues and discussions themselves in a variety of contexts.

↓ **Yes**

Have we considered specific activities that could be undertaken if a pupil is experiencing bullying because they are lesbian, gay or bisexual themselves or have family members who identify as such? → **No** → Schools should be able to respond quickly to support individuals in an appropriate, helpful and sensitive way. Developing strategies for targeted work will be useful for staff.

Figure 9.4 Developing the curriculum to prevent homophobic and biphobic bullying (Adapted from Department for Children, Schools and Families, 2007)

KEY POINTS

✓ Draw up through consultation and enshrine in practice comprehensive anti-bullying polices which make specific reference to homophobic and biphobic bullying. Ensure that each member of staff and every pupil knows how to access school policies (every school's PSHE policy should be on its website and there is no reason why your school's anti-bullying policy should not be there similarly).

✓ Let your school see that you deal as swiftly as possible with incidents of bullying, harassment or intimidation aimed at either pupils or staff.

✓ Speak and act confidently and positively when referring to sexuality issues around the school. Do not say 'gay', 'bisexual' or 'lesbian' surreptitiously to colleagues in hushed tones as if you are talking about something clandestine. Other colleagues and pupils (the latter intuit a great deal and often very accurately) will formulate opinions and draw relevant conclusions based on how you are seen to address issues of sexuality.

✓ Identify and capitalise on pupils' resilience and coping strategies. Much can be learned from 'out' lesbian, gay and bisexual pupils about their resourcefulness. From this, good practice can be put in place and policies informed. Schools need to build on what is already being effectively implemented and moreover whatever works. Speak to your 'pupils with presence' here. Every school is different. If you have a friend who teaches in another school, with thriving 'out' lesbian, gay or bisexual pupils, invite them to come and speak to staff, a year group in your school or your school's LGBT group.

✓ Utilise every opportunity to flag up in school what is expected of everyone concerning equalities, respect, anti-discrimination work and prejudice-based bullying: use Facebook, Instagram, Twitter, YouTube, TikTok (or whichever social media has now taken over from these!), posters on noticeboards, homework diaries, signs above reception, leaflets, blogs, newsletters, school prospectuses, z-cards (concertinaed fold-out cards) – the list is almost inexhaustible. Refresh the message continually so it remains contemporary, renewed, dynamic and appealing. This shows you are maintaining vigilance as a school on a number of levels.

CHAPTER 10

Anti-Bullying Policies and Creating Inclusive Environments

Anti-bullying policies are the foundation on which a safe and inclusive school environment is built. Effective policies should not only provide clear methods for dealing with reported or suspected cases of bullying but promote equality and diversity. It is vital therefore that these recognise all forms of prejudice-based bullying including homophobic and biphobic bullying. Explicit references to such bullying acknowledge it as a potential problem and provide staff with the tools to recognise and respond to it. These acknowledgements send a clear and authoritative message that homophobic bullying and name-calling will not be tolerated within your school.

Words alone however are not enough and your anti-bullying policy is only as successful as its implementation. The ethos of a policy must be embedded within the day-to-day practices of your school. For this to work, a whole-school approach should be adopted. This means involving pupils, parents, staff, support staff, governors, trustees and other key stakeholders when developing and reviewing anti-bullying policies and procedures.

Consulting with and including the whole school in the development of anti-bullying policies encourages everyone to take ownership of its implementation and establishes an inclusive culture from the outset whereby everyone's voice is valued and heard.

At Talbot Heath it is important that pupils see our equalities policy in action rather than viewing it as a document. Pupils identifying as lesbian, gay or bisexual, who hold responsibility within the school, discuss school policy with the senior team. (Angharad Holloway, Headmistress, Talbot Heath Girls School, Bournemouth)

Anti-bullying policies can too often be subject to a 'copy-and-paste' or 'off-the-shelf' approach where example policies are adopted by schools. This approach is problematic as a single anti-bullying policy will not be applicable to the diverse school contexts in which it is being used. As a result, policies conceived in this way will invariably reside on a dusty shelf unused and unread by the very people they are intended to support. Within the busy environment of a school it is understandable that such short-cuts appeal. I have been asked frequently why a 'model policy' is not available to download from EACH's website and this is why. The development of an anti-bullying policy should not be viewed as simply an administrative exercise but an opportunity to engage the whole-school environment in a conversation about how to make the school a safe, welcoming and inclusive one for all.

Governors or trustees have legal responsibility for a school's anti-bullying policy and procedures. They should be able to demonstrate that policies have been reviewed regularly and developed in consultation at least with colleagues if not with the pupils and staff of your school. If you are a governor with responsibility for behaviour or safeguarding, it is important that you can evidence how this consultation process has been undertaken.

If you are a teacher who recognises an oversight regarding homophobic or biphobic bullying within your school's policies you can raise this with your manager. It can be useful to have evidence to present to them. This could include highlighting Ofsted's guidance on your school's actions to prevent homophobic bullying and keeping a record of incidents that have caused concern (Ofsted, 2014a). Together with your manager, you can raise this issue with your senior leadership team.

If you are a parent and your school's anti-bullying policy does not explicitly reference homophobic and biphobic bullying you should raise this as an issue with the school. You can talk through concerns with your child's teacher, tutor or head of year. Alternatively, you may wish to write a letter to the headteacher. If these actions do not address your concerns you can send a letter to the chair of governors or director of trustees. If none of your interventions bring you satisfaction you may choose to write to either your local government ombudsman or to the Secretary of State for Education.

Developing an anti-bullying policy: The process

To ensure key stakeholders are represented from the outset, establish a working group to review current policies and procedures. The working group may include governors, members of the senior leadership team, learning support assitants, teachers, pupils and parents. It may also be advisable to invite an external agency with specialist and professional expertise around homophobia and biphobia to brief the group. This will ensure that the working group is appropriately resourced to address the issue of offline and online homophobic bullying within policies and procedures.

The working group should consult the whole school in order to establish:

- a common definition of bullying including homophobic and biphobic bullying

- an understanding of the extent and types of bullying that occur and where

- opportunities for reporting incidents

- expected roles and responsibilities of staff, governors, parents and pupils

- a hierarchy of sanctions to prevent and respond to bullying

- a reward system to reinforce and celebrate positive behaviour.

These discussions will inform the core of your anti-bullying policy: establishing a common understanding of bullying and how it should be dealt with by the school.

Consulting staff

Staff need to be informed and on board with developments of anti-bullying policies and procedures if they are to implement them effectively. In a 2012 study, Ofsted found that senior leadership teams had an 'overly positive' view of their colleagues' understanding and confidence concerning homophobic bullying (Ofsted, 2012, p.37). Your colleagues can be confident they are addressing these issues by completing questionnaires and training needs assessments. These should not be issued to teaching staff alone but also capture the insights of learning mentors, teaching assistants, lunchtime supervisors, site managers and administrative staff. Support staff are equally vital for ensuring that the ethos of your school's policy is embedded within day-to-day practice and for modelling an inclusive school culture.

A staff questionnaire or training needs assessment could cover:

- perspectives on homophobic and biphobic bullying in your school and how prevalent they feel it is

- understanding of different aspects of homophobic and biphobic bullying such as who experiences it, who perpetrates it and what it looks like

- experience of dealing with homophobic and biphobic bullying and how well they felt they dealt with it

- any barriers they have identified in challenging homophobic and biphobic bullying, for example linked to their own professional confidence, personal convictions, difficulty engaging with parents or problematic school procedures

- knowledge of lesbian, gay and bisexual issues and supporting sensitive disclosures

- what works, positive experiences and examples of best practice that they have witnessed in your school or others.

Analysing results from your staff consultation will help identify gaps in knowledge. It may be, for example, that teachers recognise homophobic language where it occurs but do not feel equipped to challenge it, do not recognise it or do not acknowledge it as an issue. Once you have identified areas that need attention, staff training can be tailored to meet these specific needs. Tapping into EACH or another training provider's expertise to deliver staff training can be particularly helpful for motivating and inspiring them to establish a consistent approach to homophobic and biphobic bullying.

Consulting pupils

Pupils are vital to the success of anti-bullying strategies and their voice should be at the heart of interventions. For anti-bullying initiatives to be a success, schools must establish a reporting culture whereby pupils feel confident that they can tell someone about their bullying and secure the support they need. Too often pupils fear that the bullying will not be dealt with and telling someone will only make the problem worse. If pupils are not confident that the procedures in place will be effective then more work needs to be done by the school to instil this confidence. Reviewing anti-bullying policies and procedures on a regular basis will provide an opportunity to reflect on whether this is the case in your school and identify areas for improvement. When consulting pupils, it is important to get a representative selection of pupils by age, gender and ethnicity. It is equally important to listen to all pupils and not rely too heavily on your 'pupils with presence'. Often those who are the quietest need the most help.

> Lesbian, gay and bisexual students feel well supported in [this] school and when asked if they would like a club/group, they explained that they didn't feel this was needed as they felt sufficiently supported by pastoral/teaching staff and their friends/allies. This has meant that support is woven into the wider support of students here instead of being a stand-alone separate entity. (Inner city secondary school teacher)

Interestingly this was at odds with the view of a number of lesbian, gay or bisexual pupils from this school who demonstrated, both by their eagerness to attend a consultation session and through what they said, that their school *was* in need of a regular safe space for pupils to meet and discuss matters and issues of concern. Taking the temperature of what is happening in your school through referral to 'pupils of presence' is admirable but we also need to seek out the views of the quieter pupils who are not as able or willing to proffer their opinion unless provided with the opportunity.

There are a multitude of opportunities for consulting over anti-bullying strategies. These include:

- focus groups

- face-to-face discussions with small groups of pupils across the year groups such as the school council or pupil parliament

- exploring the topic in PSHE, citizenship, politics or RSE

- completing anonymous feedback forms and questionnaires.

In Bristol, Little Mead Primary Academy's Headteacher wanted her school to revise its anti-bullying policy so invited one of the school's governors and EACH to work with small groups of children drawn from Reception to Year 6 (ages 5–11), appraising the existing policy and drafting wording for the new one in their own words. Understandably, the ultimate policy was couched in a register reflecting the top end of the primary school rather than the youngest year, but what a fantastic way to include all ages of children at a grass-roots level and what a thrill for those children to be selected to participate. They will remember this always and we hope they will hold on to the laudable reasons why the school wanted to do things this way. An illustration of part of Little Mead Primary Academy's anti-bullying policy is available in its case study.

CASE STUDY: Little Mead Primary: 'Say No to Bullying'

PURPOSE

At Little Mead Primary School, we promote the values of honesty, respect and a sense of community. We believe that every child matters and aim that all children will:

- be successful, resilient and ambitious learners

- be respectful and responsible local and global citizens

- have the aspiration, confidence and skills to continue learning beyond school.

One way in which we pursue these aims is through our positive approach to anti-bullying. We call this strategy 'Say No to Bullying'.

If children are to understand that bullying is wrong and to have the confidence to say no to bullying, they need to be able to empathise or 'stand in the shoes' of others. They need to be able to form good relationships and understand how to deal with conflict. They should understand that they have rights but also that they have responsibilities.

We are committed to providing a caring, friendly and safe environment where pupils can learn and participate in all aspects of school life. We value the self-esteem of every child. Everybody has the right to be treated with respect and bullying of any kind is unacceptable.

If bullying does occur all pupils should be able to tell an adult. We will respond promptly and effectively to issues of bullying. Pupils who bully must take responsibility for their actions and need to learn different ways of behaving.

WHAT IS BULLYING?

The following definitions have been discussed and agreed by staff, parents and pupils:

- Bullying is the use of aggression or coercion with the intention of hurting another person. Bullying is the repeated use of these things, causing distress and anxiety to the victim.

- Bullying is unkindness which you don't like and which hurts you. It is continuous and may carry on even after an adult has intervened.

Bullying can be:

- **emotional:** unfriendly, excluding, tormenting or threatening, 'ganging up'

- **verbal:** name-calling, sarcasm, spreading rumours, teasing

- **physical:** pushing, kicking, hitting, punching or any use of violence

- **racist:** racial taunts, graffiti, gestures

- **homophobic:** focusing on sexuality

- **cyber:** email and internet chat room misuse, threats by text messaging and calls.

Talking to pupils will also help your school identify pockets of excellence along with areas of practice that need attention. You can ask pupils about situations in which a response to homophobic or biphobic bullying or language was felt to be particularly effective. Similarly, if approaches to challenging such bullying are inconsistent across the school your 'pupils with presence' can tell you. You may consider working with pupils to establish a hierarchy of sanctions and rewards to deter negative behaviour and celebrate positive behaviour. This will promote a just, fair culture and pupils will be less likely to take umbrage over a sanction that they recognise has been designed by fellow pupils.

Another added benefit of consulting pupils is that they will be able to alert you to any issues arising before they become full-blown problems. Problematic behaviour online, for example, may only come to the attention of your school if it escalates into a safeguarding issue.

Consulting pupils about what they do online will proactively prevent such issues arising and allow you to understand how your pupils view and manage their own safety and wellbeing.

Consulting parents

Parents need to be consulted and feel their opinions are valued when developing school policies and procedures. This can be especially important when developing practice around a sensitive topic such as homophobic and biphobic bullying. Parents are important allies to ensuring that an inclusive school culture is promoted both inside and outside school. This requires clear and effective communication with them to ensure that they are informed of school developments.

Engaging parents can be a challenge for many schools. The less positive a parent's experience of their own schooling the less likely they are to engage with your school via their child. Primary schools will find that their parents are more involved with the school. Secondary schools however often struggle to maintain this engagement as pupils become older and more independent. There are numerous behavioural and academic benefits to continuing to engage parents with their child's school. Ofsted increasingly looks at how schools are engaging pupils' and parents' views particularly when developing e-safety strategies (Ofsted, 2014b).

Response rates to parental consultations can be variable especially if parents do not feel their opinions are valued. Parents should feel trusted and listened to by the school and a variety of techniques can be employed to open up these channels of communication. Typical avenues include formal parent–teacher meetings and annual or biennial surveys. These opportunities can be further promoted through letters home, newsletters, text messages, email reminders, social media call-outs and prize draws. These methods should not only be used to elicit parental views but also to feed back to parents about the findings of consultations. Regardless of whether messages are positive or critical you should be willing to discuss results with your school and provide detailed plans of action. This will demonstrate to parents and the school more widely that their views were listened to and the school is taking proactive action. This not only helps build better relationships between your school and its parents but may encourage parents to offer their specific expertise or support to anti-bullying working groups.

A number of parents at the school may be lesbian, gay or bisexual and will wish and need to feel represented within your policies and procedures. Utilising inclusive language within general school communications is a great opportunity to demonstrate that all parents are valued 'family members' of the school. Actively invite lesbian, gay or bisexual parents to join your school's board of governors or trustees. This will send a positive and powerful message to the entire school about how much you value different families. Your school will gain hugely from an informed, articulate gay, lesbian or bisexual parent.

Writing the policy

Schools should involve the whole school in agreeing the definition of bullying so that the issue is understood and owned by everybody. Your school's definition should be suitably child friendly and accessible according to the age and ability of the pupils. Box 10.1 outlines a structure that could be used for an anti-bullying policy.

Be clear on the audience for your policy. It may be necessary to develop a suite of differentiated policies that are accessible and workable documents for governors, teaching staff, pupils and parents.

Box 10.1: Anti-bullying policy

Purpose
Make a positive and inclusive statement about the school and that bullying will not be tolerated.

Definition
Agree a common and accessible definition of bullying with your pupils. Remember to include details of types of bullying behaviour for example physical, verbal, relational or material. Also include details of types of prejudice-based bullying such as homophobic, racist and disablist.

Reporting bullying
Explain to pupils what they should do if they are a target of bullying or they witness bullying. Also explain how they can expect school staff to respond should they report an incident of bullying and detail the hierarchy of sanctions in place for bullying incidents.

It may also be apposite to include information for parents here on what they can do if their child is being bullied. Alternatively, this can be issued as a supplementary document.

Recording bullying
Include a statement about confidentiality here along with details of where bullying reports will be recorded and who is responsible for this system. You should also explain how this information will be used so that pupils understand why the information is being recorded.

Strategies for preventing bullying
Explain the initiatives and strategies in place at the school to prevent bullying from occurring and to promote an inclusive ethos.

Promoting the policy

Once the anti-bullying policy has been published ensure that you promote it widely and celebrate the achievements of those who contributed to its formation. You can communicate and disseminate the anti-bullying policy across the school by:

- discussing it with pupils during tutorial time or registration

- assigning dedicated staff training to the new policy and what it means for school practice

- informing parents of the policy via parent–teacher meetings or school newsletters.

In order to celebrate the achievements of those involved in creating the policy, and to ensure it is promoted with some fanfare, host an anti-bullying launch involving the whole school. This will help elevate the policy and the valuable work that has gone into creating it. Celebrating the success helps affirm your school's positive ethos and assures everyone that everybody at the school is valued and equal.

KEY POINTS

✓ Anti-bullying policies are the bedrock of work in challenging homophobic and biphobic bullying and building safe and inclusive school environments.

✓ The ethos of a policy must be embedded within the day-to-day practices of the school.

✓ Everyone in the school should be consulted when developing an anti-bullying policy: not least the pupils.

✓ Be clear on the audience for your policy ensuring that it is accessible and relevant for governors, teaching staff, pupils and parents.

✓ Celebrate the policy at every opportunity and review it regularly to ensure that procedures are effective and up to date.

CHAPTER 11

Frequently Asked Questions

1. What is homophobia?

Homophobia is a resentment or fear of lesbian, gay and bisexual people. At its most benign it is voiced as a passive dislike of gay people. At its worst it involves active victimisation: targeting an individual in direct or indirect ways. Homophobia can also affect people perceived to be lesbian, gay or bisexual, someone who has an association with gay people or someone who does not conform to stereotypical expectations of masculine or feminine behaviour.

2. What is biphobia?

Many hours of interviews have contributed to the writing of this book informed by engagement with hundreds of pupils and their teachers in schools reflecting various settings – urban, rural and suburban. One of the many interesting revelations transpiring from these interviews was the number of pupils who identified as bisexual. Biphobic bullying is intriguing since biphobic name-calling is much less frequent (and actually harder to 'do' given that there are fewer slurs directed explicitly at bisexual people than at lesbian or gay people) than homophobic name-calling. Biphobia is delivered more through actions such as ostracism or derogatory laughter rather than insulting words.

Pupils regularly cited having to explain or defend bisexuality to peers and if explanations were considered inadequate the individual was deemed to be 'making it up', showboating or to actually be gay or lesbian but unprepared to 'confess' this. For this reason, when your school or other young people's setting is looking to challenge homophobic bullying bear in mind biphobic bullying and name-calling because there are as many bisexual or questioning pupils who need support as there are gay or lesbian pupils.

3. What is transphobia?

Transphobia describes the aggression or negativity directed at a transgender person. This can range from jokes, graffiti, insults and threats to physical attacks. Transgender is the umbrella term for people who identify with a gender other than that assigned to them at birth. The term can be acceptably abbreviated to 'trans'.

4. Is being gay the problem?

It is not being gay that makes some young people unhappy. It is the negative reaction of other people that they fear and coming to terms with being 'different' that is difficult. It is even harder if this has to be done in secrecy, hidden from family, friends and teachers. Lesbian, gay and bisexual people of all ages can find themselves emotionally exhausted by having to reconcile how they feel inside with the problems others have in coming to terms with their sexuality.

5. Is it appropriate to tell 'out' pupils, 'effeminate' boys or 'masculine' girls to be more discreet to avoid bullying?

No. Telling a pupil to be more discreet suggests the bullying is their fault and they are 'bringing it on themselves', and it undermines their identity. Removing the target rather than responding to the bullying itself will not solve the problem. Schools need to work with pupils who engage in homophobic bullying to ensure they understand that their behaviour is unacceptable, the impact of their actions, and that they must make amends for the damage caused. Pupils experiencing bullying need to be worked with to help them develop coping strategies and resilience.

6. But will I need to talk about sex if I'm challenging or supporting a pupil regarding homophobic or biphobic bullying?

Addressing homophobic bullying and sexual orientation equality does not mean discussing sex. It means taking decisive and assertive action to prevent bullying and promote equality. Sexual orientation is distinct from sexual behaviour and refers to the combination of one's emotional, sexual and physical attraction to someone of the opposite, same or either sex. Neither heterosexual nor same-sex relationships are defined solely by sex. Just as schools are able to discuss heterosexual relationships without referring to sex, it is equally possible to discuss same-sex relationships.

RSE has an important role to play in challenging many of the myths and misconceptions that underlie homophobic prejudice. Under the Equality Act 2010 schools have a legal duty to ensure that teaching is accessible to all pupils, including those who are lesbian, gay or bisexual. An RSE curriculum which includes inclusive and age-appropriate conversations about the emotional, social and physical aspects of same-sex relationships will complement and reinforce work in challenging homophobic and biphobic bullying.

7. We have to respect cultural and religious differences. Does this mean that pupils can be homophobic?

No. It is true that some religions or cultures are not very, or at all, inclusive or tolerant of same-sex relationships. This is never a justification for homophobic bullying. An individual has a right to believe what they want but it is unacceptable for an individual to express their views in a way that degrades others. If a pupil engages in persistent bullying due to their cultural or religious traditions contacting their parents to alert them to the issue will be necessary and sanctions will be required.

There is a strong legal and moral imperative for educators to challenge homophobia whenever it occurs just as there is an imperative to challenge racist or faith-based prejudice wherever this occurs. Anyone can experience homophobic bullying regardless of their sexual orientation, religion, culture or national identity and all deserve to be protected. Educating pupils about our religious, cultural and national differences can be a great platform for celebrating diversity of all kinds. Respect, empathy and kindness should be integral to the ethos of every school.

8. Is all this relevant to pupils with additional or special educational needs?

Too often pupils with additional or special educational needs do not have their sexuality issues addressed and it is invariably assumed they are heterosexual. It is important however, that these pupils have access to appropriate information, advice and guidance around sexual orientation and that teachers in special schools recognise that support needs for pupils who are coming out are differentiated proportionately for pupils with additional needs.

9. Is the phrase 'That's SO gay!' homophobic?

Over the years EACH has worked with many gay and heterosexual people who are upset and frustrated by the persistent use of 'gay' as a derogatory term. This use of language does not always equate to bullying as many young people use it to refer to an inanimate object or an unwelcome situation. Nevertheless, it is a 'micro-aggression' reinforcing on a daily basis the idea that being gay is somehow stupid, pathetic, rubbish or wrong. This language sends an undermining, negative message to gay young people paving the way for serious mental health issues.

10. What about dissenting parents?

No parent wants their child to be bullied nor do most wish to hear that their child is a bully. Regardless of their views on gay people, or sexual orientation in general, parents need to recognise that your school has a legal responsibility to keep every pupil safe from harm. Preventing and responding to homophobic bullying is crucial if your school is to fulfil its responsibilities. Parents should be involved in your school's consultations on this topic and contribute to ways in which it can be stopped. Parents also need to acknowledge that any pupil can be affected by homophobic bullying regardless of their sexuality.

11. Is this an issue for primary-age pupils?

I have taught and worked in hundreds of primary and secondary schools since 1985 and this has evidenced very clearly to me that the average seven-year-old understands that gay people 'exist' because they learn this from television or they have a sibling, aunt, cousin, godparent or family friend who is lesbian, gay or bisexual who they are quite happy to talk to you about if you wish them to. Primary school pupils will be too young to know their own sexual orientation but many will know someone who is gay. Homophobic language is used in primary schools without our pupils necessarily understanding what it is that they are saying. If you are a primary school teacher the same strategies you use to deal with other forms of inappropriate language should be deployed here. Simply respond to homophobic language as you would when a child says something offensive but you know they do understand what they have said. Age appropriately, you explain what is and is not acceptable in your school.

12. Am I allowed to be out as a lesbian, gay or bisexual teacher?

Your school's ethos and staffroom culture will determine how open it wishes you to be about your sexual orientation and you would be advised to seek guidance from your headteacher in the first instance. The key is consistency and fairness among all staff regardless of sexual orientation. See Part Two of Personal and Professional Conduct in *Teachers' Standards: Guidance for School Leaders, School Staff and Governing Bodies* (Department for Education, 2013) for more information. Pupils, especially lesbian, gay or bisexual pupils, will benefit from knowing positive role models who are out. All staff should ensure that they provide advice and guidance objectively and without bias.

13. Should I do or say anything about a pupil I teach being gay?

There is no incumbency on you to quiz any pupil about their sexual orientation or insinuate in your conversations with them that you are concerned that they may be gay. If a pupil chooses to come out to you it is important to be upbeat. That way, they will be more likely to tell you if they are concerned about anything including coming out or bullying. Developing a school ethos where all your pupils feel respected is essential for giving your pupils the assurance to talk to you if they need to.

14. Why is this relevant? We have no lesbian, gay or bisexual pupils at our school

You have, therefore it is. In an average sized secondary school of 1200 pupils, at a conservative estimate statistically 36 will identify as gay or bisexual in adulthood (even if only to themselves). That's roughly the equivalent of one tutor group. Some will be coming out in a year or two's time and many will enter same-sex relationships. Furthermore, homophobic or biphobic bullying can affect anyone regardless of sexual orientation. Anyone who is thought to be gay or just thought to be different can be called gay or experience homophobic abuse. Even if a pupil is not lesbian, gay or bisexual they may have close family members or friends who are and this is relevant to all of these pupils. Finally, there are gay people in the wider world (including, of course, the teachers in their school who may or may not be out) and therefore challenging homophobic bullying is essential to your pupils' wider education.

15. How should I treat the lesbian, gay or bisexual parents at my school?

Treat them like any other parent. Biological and non-biological parents have the same rights and responsibilities. Non-biological parents have the same rights as step-parents and may adopt the child or apply for a parental responsibility giving them the same legal responsibility as a biological parent. It is important that schools treat all parents in the same manner and they feel invited to be part of school life and activities. Your school will benefit from actively encouraging engagement with a diverse range of parents.

16. Where do we stand concerning homophobic or biphobic bullying outside school?

Your school is partially responsible for bullying taking place outside school (including cyberbullying) in addition to taking steps to challenge bullying inside school. It must be responsive to incidents which happen when pupils are in uniform on their way to and from your school. This can be on foot, public transport or in local shops. Under the UK's Education and Inspection Act 2006 a school's behaviour policy can include measures to discipline poor behaviour both on and off school premises. For more detail see the *Behaviour and Discipline in Schools: Advice for Headteachers and School Staff* (Department for Education, 2016).

17. Should I reflect the terminology a pupil uses in a conversation about themselves which feels inappropriate?

Young people have many ways to describe their sexual orientation and some may use terms like queer or dyke to describe this. If you are more used to hearing terms like heterosexual, lesbian, gay or bisexual and there are words which make you feel uncomfortable for any reason, feel at liberty to ask your young person what they mean by any term so you understand and can speak with them more confidently and helpfully. If you are unhappy repeating a descriptor, with which they identify, simply don't and certainly avoid repeating or using terms you do not understand.

18. Is it a good idea to set up a LGBT+ group in my school?

Schools where EACH works which have an LGBT+ group are invariably places where pupils feel safer and have faith in their teachers to care for everyone's wellbeing. Such a group can give pupils the opportunity to voice concerns about school issues and suggest ideas which can help pastorally and academically so staff know what positive changes need to be made. Lesbian, gay, bisexual or gender-questioning pupils are far more likely to stay on at your school when it has an LGBT+ group. Both staff and pupils feel more empowered to challenge homophobic, biphobic or transphobic bullying and LGBT+ staff will feel more valued and affirmed.

19. What's the simplest way to introduce the topic of same-sex relationships, age appropriately, into any curriculum subject?

Where you would ordinarily use a boy and girl in any scenario involving a pair make it girls or boys. For example, in a maths or modern languages problem, two men could go to the shop to purchase apples rather than a man and a woman. If your pupils ask anything about the relationship between the two it opens up the potential for discussion. They could be siblings, friends, partners. The latter, met with any giggling or inappropriateness, can be responded to as you see fit (see previous chapters for ideas). A conversation might be had about how often we see stereotyped illustrations of couples being a man and woman especially in advertising. This is the one idea which pupils informing this book unanimously agreed was the best first step.

20. Are things getting better or worse concerning homophobic and biphobic bullying?

Better. In the last five years, changes in the law have created protections for both adults and children regarding sexual orientation matters. The Relationships and Sex Education (LGBT inclusive) curriculum is mandatory as of September 2020: reinforcing all your anti-bullying practice. Polls can cite escalations in homophobic crime or bullying but do not become despondent. Surveys are demographic dependent and do not always provide the most accurate picture. There are children in schools right across the UK who need our support to help them realise their sexuality or recognise that they are experiencing homophobic or biphobic bullying. We have a duty to put a stop to this subjectively and contribute to effecting this throughout the school. There are a myriad of resources available to help you do this – so approach it collectively in liaison with your senior leadership team and governors.

CHAPTER 12

Last Words

I trust this book has prompted some valuable thinking about ways you can recognise, stop and prevent homophobic and biphobic bullying in your setting. On EACH's website you will find some resources which should prove useful in your classroom or activity space. I would also like to leave you with some points on which to reflect. They are informed by my years as a teacher, trainer and consultant working variously with teachers, the Department for Education, schools, colleges and universities, Ofsted, the Government Equalities Office, the major teaching unions, the police service, the College of Policing, the National Crime Agency, the Crown Prosecution Service, the Prison Service, the National Health Service, doctors, nurses, council officials, youth workers and others.

I distinctly remember my A-level English teacher telling me, as we studied George Orwell's *1984*, that if we change the way we speak, we change the way we think. I remain firmly convinced this is entirely true. The importance of adopting appropriate vocabulary when promoting equality and diversity cannot be understated. Language is a powerful tool. When deployed negatively it reinforces stereotypes and discrimination. It also has the power to debunk stereotypes, explode myths and eliminate misconceptions.

So, here are some words, phrases and concepts on which you may care to reflect as you pledge to undertake work to challenge homophobic and biphobic bullying or support a child who would benefit from a conversation about same-sex relationships as these impinge on their family. Perhaps you are eager to support a young person who comes out to you as lesbian, gay or bisexual (or who is already out).

Heterosexual – straight – homosexual – gay

Those who are in the majority in society enjoy a privileged social status – such as being heterosexual – and are invariably described in terms which reinforce such status. The word 'straight' to mean heterosexual is a classic example. 'Straight' means uniform, direct, level, upright and properly positioned. Whenever it is employed to refer to someone's heterosexuality it underpins their position as 'normal' and thus differentiates heterosexual people from those whose sexuality is seen to be 'abnormal': bent, deviant, inverted or improper: bisexual, lesbian, gay.

It is this implication by some that lesbian, gay or bisexual people are 'abnormal' which leads into the trap of talking about such people as having a 'sexual preference', inclination, proclivity or tendency. We never, ever refer to heterosexual people as having an inclination, a proclivity or a tendency. Heterosexual people do not come to the realisation they are heterosexual or choose to be. They simply are.

The use of such terms is not only patronising and disrespectful but carries a number of implications. All three words refer to someone's predisposition to feel, act or behave in a certain way. When we refer to someone's 'homosexual tendencies' we often reduce gay people to certain feelings, actions and behaviours. Inclination, proclivity and tendency carry innuendo: insinuating something is warped or 'out of true'.

Heterosexual fits within the family of words describing sexual orientation – heterosexual, lesbian, gay and bisexual – and which you will find used consistently by government and the Criminal Justice System. We can therefore avoid language which 'reduces' lesbian, gay or bisexual people by using the words heterosexual, bisexual, lesbian and gay consistently.

In many instances, the use, or as I see it misuse, of the word 'homosexual' (instead of gay) and indeed 'straight' (instead of heterosexual) arises from genuine ignorance about the effect of such words on particular listeners or readers. 'Heterosexual' was coined the same time as the word 'homosexual' in the mid-19th century by an Austro-Hungarian journalist named Károly Mária Kertbeny. While heterosexual went on to have no negative connotations whatsoever (and indeed not one derogatory synonym aside from 'breeder'), homosexual coined a plethora of (almost entirely negative) synonyms reflecting society's disapproval of the sexual orientation and all things associated with it. The only neutral or positive synonym for homosexual is 'gay'. Heterosexual has no negative synonyms reflecting society's approval of the sexual orientation it is describing. Compare this with those scores of alternatives for homosexual almost all of which are deeply offensive to many lesbian, gay and bisexual people, their loved ones and allies.

> People don't realise the history of the derogatory words they use. If they did I think they would never use them! (Lucy, 16)

As Gary Nunn comments in his article 'A challenge to the Guardian: it's time to drop the word "homosexual"' (Nunn, 2011), in order to stop homophobic and biphobic bullying, lesbian, gay and bisexual people need to be normalised by language – not distanced by it. Plain English dictates that we use 'people' instead of homo sapiens so it follows that 'gay people' is less stigmatising than 'homosexuals'. The noun 'homosexual' is equally dehumanising and cold.

There is a deeper, more important reason to scrap this pernicious noun, he continues. I agree with Nunn when he says that it is loaded with discriminatory baggage. 'Homosexual' readily came to be the carefully chosen oppressive medical vernacular employed to describe gay people as mentally ill. The American Psychiatric Association officially declassified it as a mental illness in 1974 but the World Health Organization not until as late as 1992. The hangover effect, however, lives on – some medical professionals still use it as a justification for carrying out so-called 'homosexual cure' therapies.

Historically our biggest state institutions of Church, Health, Criminal Justice System and Education have all at times used homosexual to denote disapproval or to sanction lesbian, gay or bisexual people. 'Homosexuality is a sin' is an oft seen position from certain quarters of the Christian Church and other world faiths. The 'AIDS epidemic' of the 1980s and 1990s saw the tabloid press frenziedly referring to 'homosexuals' and a 'gay plague' while until the introduction of the Sexual Offences Act 2003 the Criminal Justice System regularly conflated the word homosexual with criminal activity. Making up the quartet, the introduction of the pernicious Section 28 of the Local Government Act 1988 saw 'homosexuality' described as 'a pretended family relationship'. As such, 'homosexual' can never be thought to come from a neutral position.

Gay community – heterosexual community

We never refer to the 'heterosexual community' so why do we refer to the 'gay community'? It always makes the speaker sound as if they are talking about a group of people to which they do not belong and who are uniform in their values and beliefs. From this, it is a quick step to talking about 'gays' adopting the 'homosexual lifestyle', two other really unhelpful expressions. The police service uses 'the gay community' all the time and in my training and consultancy with the Criminal Justice System, I encourage them to understand why expressions such as 'people who are gay' or 'individuals who are gay' are far more respectful than the 'gay community'.

When, at a conference at which we shared the same platform, I asked a black woman and a disabled gold medal-winning Paralympian, 'Do you mind being referred to as members of the black and disabled community respectively?' They instantly and loudly voiced their antipathy towards these labels and stated that they were individuals and resented being 'all lumped together as members of some so-called community'. Interestingly, spontaneous applause erupted from the predominantly white, able-bodied, heterosexual audience.

Just gay

So often we see expressions in the tabloid press like 'openly gay' or 'admitting one is gay' as if it is some sort of guilty secret to which one has confessed. It is never helpful to pluralise groups of people and describe them as, for example, Jews, the deaf or gays. It dehumanises people and makes any 'group' much easier to dismiss or demonise. Simply adding 'people' after the noun demonstrates respect and accords people value: thus 'Jewish people' or 'people who are gay'. Someone's entire identity cannot be reduced to a single characteristic. Gay people are not defined by their sexuality.

Target – bully – hate crime – prejudice-based crime

I use 'target' consistently in my work, never 'victim'. A target is not necessarily hit. It can move. It can be missed. Victim has no synonym. It is a disempowering word with connotations of resignation and defeatism. Similarly, in my work with the Criminal Justice System I cringe whenever I hear individuals described as having been 'the victim of a hate crime'. Not all hate crimes are actually motivated by hate. Some arise from ignorance and lack of knowledge. Would a target of such a crime not feel so much more empowered about their situation were they to be described as having been 'the target of prejudice-based crime'? I believe so and I use this expression always because of this. In schools we talk about prejudice-based bullying not 'hate bullying'. Yet the adult phrase 'hate crime' (which we have imported from the USA) continues to be the one adhered to by our Criminal Justice System. Once again, through my years of work with agencies from the National Crime Agency and College of Policing to the Crown Prosecution Service and police service, I can see positive headway having been made in fostering an awareness of the advantages of using language which appeals to targets of bullying or crime rather than victims of hate. Think therefore about using target instead of victim in your language describing bullying. It is bullying behaviour too which we are describing in our perpetrator. For this reason, it is a really good idea not to call the pupil 'a bully'. The word 'bully' is like a sticker. It labels people as something. They are someone who, at the present time, bullies. What they do is demonstrate bullying behaviour. If we write them off as a bully they are far less likely to believe they can stop or to bother trying.

One final thought – when we reduce people to TLAs (three letter abbreviations!) such as LGB it is too easy to stop thinking of them as people and certainly as individuals. Yes, it takes longer to say out loud 'lesbian, gay or bisexual people' but it is undeniably more inclusive and respectful. To avoid constant repetition in, for instance, policies or documents, one would expect to see LGB used (as in this book's appendices) but always use lesbian, gay or bisexual the first time round so its use is clear. I notice similarly that we are moving from BME (black and minority ethnic) as an abbreviation to BAME (black, Asian and minority ethnic). It is just something about which to open up a conversation with colleagues, friends and family as relevant.

Conclusion

Remember each of us has, as an adult, not only power and influence but also the moral duty to do what we can to challenge homophobic and biphobic name-calling and bullying. I trust this book provides you with hands-on, practical guidance as to how to develop an holistic yet dynamic approach to this work. Let us hope a book on how to recognise, stop and prevent transphobic bullying is written soon.

Throughout the course of this book I have explored a range of topics and ideas which I hope will help you and your school to better challenge and prevent homophobic and biphobic bullying. This is an issue that has widespread impact on young people regardless of their sexual orientation and cannot be underestimated. Get this right and you will definitely find other prejudice-based bullying becoming routinely easier with which to deal.

Thank you again to everyone in schools who gave up their time and energy so eagerly to inform this book's writing and all at EACH for their ongoing support of work to both challenge homophobic and biphobic bullying, inspiring schools everywhere to support their lesbian, gay and bisexual pupils and families.

Section 28 of The Local Government Act 1988

Section 28 of the Local Government Act 1988 was enacted to prevent local authorities from 'promoting homosexuality' and offering financial assistance to those 'promoting homosexuality'. The Section read as follows:

2A –

1. A local authority shall not –

    a. intentionally promote homosexuality or publish material with the intention of promoting homosexuality;

    b. promote the teaching in any maintained school of the acceptability of homosexuality as a pretended family relationship;

2. Nothing in subsection (1) above shall be taken to prohibit the doing of anything for the purpose of treating or preventing the spread of disease.

3. In any proceedings in connection with the application of this section a court shall draw such inferences as to the intention of the local authority as may reasonably be drawn from the evidence before it.

4. In subsection (1)(b) above 'maintained school' means –

    a. in England and Wales, a county school, voluntary school, nursery school or special school, within the meaning of the [Education Act 1996]; and

b. in Scotland, a public school, nursery school or special school, within the meaning of the Education (Scotland) Act 1980.

As this provision is part of civil law, actions by local authorities can be challenged only by judicial review; usually an injunction or prohibiting order is issued to restrain the authority from continuing with its action.

The Bill received Royal Assent on 24 March 1988. Attempts to repeal Section 28 were implemented in election manifestos by the Labour Party in 1992 and the Liberal Democrat Party in 1997. Despite successive defeats to repeal Section 28 in the House of Lords, the Labour Government successfully passed the Local Government Act 2003 with the effect of abolishing this provision.

The impact of Section 28

No local authority was taken to court in breach of Section 28. The impact of the legislation nevertheless cannot be underestimated. Section 28 was never directly applicable to schools because it was targeted at local councils. Compounded by continual, erroneous reinforcement by sections of the media however many working in education were under the misapprehension that it was. They felt inhibited about what they could and could not say regarding sexuality. Most schools felt constrained in their abilities to challenge homophobic and biphobic bullying. Consequently, Section 28 served to undermine the confidence of those professionals who sought and had responsibilities to provide appropriate advice and support to all young people and colleagues, especially lesbian, gay and bisexual people on the subject of same-sex relationships.

The legacy of Section 28

The repeal of Section 28 in 2003 was a watershed moment not only in terms of equalities legislation but also as a barrier to social change.

Since its repeal there has been more positive legislation and policy initiatives implemented particularly regarding challenging homophobic bullying. However, the cast of Section 28's shadow did not end with its repeal in 2003. Confusion continued to abound among many education professionals about what they could and could not say concerning sexuality largely because the 2003 Labour Government specifically requested that political lobbying organisations refrain from trumpeting its repeal, fearful as it was at the time of a backlash from elements of the right-wing tabloid press. Indeed, in 2004, Bristol City Council was the only local authority in the UK to issue specific guidance to its schools on the implications of the repeal of the legislation and what it meant for their practice, commissioning me to write *Out of the Shadow* (Charlesworth, 2004).

The enduring influence of Section 28 on school practice was highlighted during the summer of 2013 when 44 schools across England were found to include statements prohibiting the 'promotion of homosexuality' in their sex and relationship education policies (Russell, 2013).

RSE Guidelines and Homophobic and Biphobic Bullying

In April 2019, the Department for Education passed regulations to implement mandatory Relationships Education in primary schools and Relationships and Sex Education in secondary schools which will come into effect in September 2020. These regulations pertain to all schools including maintained, non-maintained or independent schools, and academies and free schools, non-maintained special schools, maintained special schools and alternative provision including pupil referral units.

In primary schools, mandatory Relationships Education must demonstrate that families of many forms provide a nurturing environment for children. These families include families with one or more parents who are gay, lesbian or bisexual. Children must be taught that others' families, either in school or in the wider world, sometimes look different from their own family but that they should respect those differences and know that other children's families are also characterised by love and care.

Furthermore, schools must educate children about different types of bullying (including cyberbullying), the impact of bullying, responsibilities of bystanders and how to get help, what a stereotype is, and how stereotypes can be unfair, negative or destructive.

In secondary schools, pupils should be taught the facts and the law about sex, sexuality, sexual health and gender identity in an age-appropriate and inclusive way. All pupils should feel that the content is relevant to them and their developing sexuality. Sexual orientation and gender identity should be explored in a clear, sensitive and respectful manner. When teaching about these topics it must be recognised that young people may be discovering or understanding their sexual orientation or gender identity. There should be an equal opportunity to explore the features of stable and healthy lesbian, gay and bisexual relationships. This should be integrated appropriately into the RSE programme rather than addressed separately or in only one lesson.

Again, teachers must explore the topic of bullying in these classes. Teachers must address how stereotypes, in particular stereotypes based on gender, race, religion, sexual orientation or disability, can cause damage (e.g. how they might normalise non-consensual behaviour or encourage prejudice).

What does this mean for teachers?

The new RSE teaching must conform to the Public Sector Equality Duty released in 2011 which aims to:

- eliminate discrimination, harassment, victimisation and any other conduct that is prohibited by or under the Equality Act 2010

- advance equality of opportunity between people who share a relevant protected characteristic and people who do not share it

- foster good relations between people who share a relevant protected characteristic and people who do not share it.

Schools should be aware of issues such as everyday sexism, misogyny, homophobia and gender stereotypes and take positive action to build a culture where these are not tolerated and any occurrences are identified and tackled.

Schools should have in place appropriate policies on bullying with explicit and detailed reference to homophobic bullying.

(Adapted from the Department for Education's *Statutory Guidance on Relationships Education, Relationships and Sex Education (RSE) and Health Education* (2019a), available in full at www.gov.uk.)

Department for Education Guidelines for Primary Schools Facing Protests Against New RSE Curriculum

Part one: Advice for early signs of co-ordinated campaign targeted at one or more schools

First step: ensure knowledge of the facts – read up on all relevant documents from the Department for Education (full list on gov.com website).

Next steps 1: look into various support mechanisms available to the school.

Next steps 2: local authority-wide activities (collaboration with faith leaders/LGBT groups/council members/police, etc.).

Next steps 3: consider possible legal response to school 1: consider safeguarding issues posed by the protest.

Next steps 4: consider possible legal response 2: this applies if the protests become disruptive and steps could include securing an injunction or public space protection order.

Part two: Advice when active disruption of the activities of one or more schools is under way

First steps: establishing process for communicating with school(s) concerned it is important that school(s) experiencing any disruptive activities feels supported and that they have a ready source of advice and guidance.

Steps that aim to reduce impact of disruption/bring it to an end: holding meetings with protestors or faith leaders, taking enforcement action against the parents for unauthorised absence, liaising with the police to understand their plans to monitor the protests and take action in the case of suspected criminal behaviour.

Steps that aim to support school(s): support for staff and pupils, support to encourage parental engagement by the school, a council worker working with the school.

Steps that aim to communicate effectively and appropriately: we recommend that local authorities put a careful communications plan in place to deal with media coverage, some of which is likely to be sensationalist and inflammatory.

Part three: Intelligence-sharing and support available

Intel and support: pass on intel to the Department for Education about disquiet in your local area and signs that this might be building towards disruptive activity – contact the Department for Education or Local Government Association to submit intel, and for support.

(Adapted from Department for Education guidance on *Primary school disruption over LGBT teaching/relationships education* (2019), available in full at www.gov.uk.)

Senior Leadership Team Guidance

Section 1: Why focus on homophobic and biphobic bullying, and lesbian, gay and bisexual inclusion?

Bullying is an issue which affects pupils and staff in schools across the country. It is cited by the Children's Society as a key reason that the UK is one of the worst countries for children and young people's life satisfaction and is something that continues to impact on people long after they leave education (2019).

Online spaces and social media provide ever-increasing opportunities for bullying which schools struggle to regulate. At the same time growing positive representation of lesbian, gay and bisexual people in mass media means youth can be more aware of their identity at a younger age. Both factors make them increasingly likely to turn to their school as a place where they hope to be understood and supported. A focus on bullying and how to recognise, stop and prevent it has never been more vital.

Schools who adopt a proactive and optimistic approach towards challenging homophobic and biphobic language and bullying get the best results. Children who feel they are safe to learn without being bullied are happier and healthier, are more likely to stay in school and continue through education and are more likely to achieve academically. Schools who work holistically to champion equality can have immeasurable impact on all areas of output.

Section 2: What outputs should I expect for my school?

Working to ensure your school environment is inclusive of lesbian, gay and bisexual pupils can lead to many positive changes in your whole-school community. Each school with whom EACH works achieves different outputs depending on their starting point. Here are some of the changes you can expect to see.

School leadership

- School leaders and governors hold a team meeting to undertake a comprehensive self-assessment and work together to set the vision and ambition for the school's work on LGB matters and equality more widely.

- A dedicated school leader, governor and staff member are appointed to champion LGB equality matters at the school.

- LGB equality champions attend external training and cascade learning to colleagues through team meetings or in-service training days.

Policy development

- Policies pertinent to equality and diversity, anti-bullying and safeguarding are updated to better affirm LGB inclusion. For example, the anti-bullying policy is updated to include specific reference to homophobic and biphobic bullying.

Teaching and learning

- Equalities and diversity matters, including LGB inclusion, are established as a standing agenda item in departmental and pastoral team meetings. Topics addressed may be inclusive vocabulary checks, resource sharing or action planning.

- A hub of resources is developed with and for teaching staff including lesson ideas and strategies for embedding LGB inclusion across the curriculum.

Pupils

- An LGB club is established for pupils to be together, talk and organise activities around the school.

- A team of pupils is supported to plan and resource lessons on LGB matters, develop a visual LGB equality campaign around the school and/or lead an assembly on the topic.

- Pupil-led fundraising and awareness-raising challenges support local and national LGB equality organisations.

School environment and pastoral systems

- Dedicated visual display boards promote affirmative LGB messages and educate about inclusive relationships.

- More books aimed at LGB or questioning pupils or written by LGB authors are added to the school library.

- Extra-curricular clubs and support services are audited to review whether activities are only reaching particular pupils at the school and plans to address barriers to participation are put in place.

Partnership working with parents, carers and local communities

- A 'Parent Cafe' consultation event is held to open up a conversation about the use of LGB inclusive books and curriculum resources.

- A regular space in the parents' newsletter is reserved for sharing updates on the school's equalities work.

- Parents are invited to a Celebrating Difference assembly in connection with an annual awareness raising date (e.g. LGBT History Month, Anti-Bullying Week, International Human Rights Day).

- Local community groups are invited to deliver talks or host a stall at school events such as assemblies, parents' evenings and staff team meetings.

Section 3: Why is this work important?

All schools in England have a legal, as well as ethical duty to ensure that children and young people under their care feel safe and included. There are specific policies and guidance in place to address discrimination that causes inequalities for pupils, parents and staff including on the grounds of perceived or actual sexual orientation or gender identity. In England there are specific policies and guidance which are designed to address discrimination that causes inequality, safeguard children and young people as well as promote their right to feel safe and live free from harm.

TABLE A4.1: RELEVANT LEGISLATION

DOCUMENT	TYPE	QUOTE	SUMMARY OF RELEVANCE
Equality Act 2010	Law	'Sexual orientation means a person's sexual orientation toward (a) persons of the same sex, (b) persons of the opposite sex, or (c) persons of either sex.' 'A person has the protected characteristic of gender reassignment if the person is proposing to undergo, is undergoing or has undergone a process (or part of a process) for the purpose of reassigning the person's sex by changing physiological or other attributes of sex.'	The Equality Act 2010 legally protects people from discrimination at work, school or in wider society by: • setting out the different ways in which it is unlawful to treat someone • detailing who is protected from discrimination, the types of discrimination under the law and what action can be taken if someone is being unfairly discriminated against • affirming that public bodies such as schools have a responsibility to proactively eliminate discrimination, advance equality of opportunity and foster good relations between different people when carrying out their activities.
Education and Inspections Act 2006	Law	'The headteacher of a relevant school must determine measures to be taken with a view to encouraging good behaviour and respect for others on the part of pupils and, in particular, preventing all forms of bullying among pupils.'	The Education and Inspections Act 2006 details schools' statutory obligations in relation to behaviour which establish clear responsibilities to prevent and respond to all forms of bullying.

Cont.

DOCUMENT	TYPE	QUOTE	SUMMARY OF RELEVANCE
Children Act 2004	Law	'The Children's Commissioner has the function of promoting awareness of the views and interests of children in England; they may encourage persons exercising functions or engaged in activities affecting children to take account of their views and interests.'	The Children Act 2004 states that the interests of children and young people are paramount in all considerations of welfare and safeguarding and that safeguarding children is everyone's responsibility. Safeguarding in the broadest sense can only be achieved by improving a wide range of outcomes for children and young people, including their health, education and development, safety and economic circumstances. This Act's ultimate purpose is to make the UK better and safer for children of all ages. The idea behind the Act is to promote (coordination) between multiple official entities to improve the overall wellbeing of children.
Ofsted Framework 2019	Guidance	An outstanding school is one in which the 'school's open culture actively promotes all aspects of pupils' welfare. Pupils are safe and feel safe at all times. They understand how to keep themselves and others safe in different situations and settings. They trust leaders to take rapid and appropriate action to resolve any concerns they have.'	The Ofsted Inspection Framework sets out how inspectors assess the behaviour and safety of pupils at the school including: • viewing records and analysis of bullying, discriminatory and prejudicial behaviour, either directly or indirectly, including racist, sexist, disability and homophobic bullying, use of derogatory language and racist incidents • gathering evidence from a wide range of pupils, both formally and informally, about their experiences of learning and behaviour, the prevention of bullying and how the school deals with discrimination and prejudiced behaviour • conducting meetings with parents, staff and other stakeholders • assessing whether teachers and other adults promote clear messages about the impact of bullying and prejudiced behaviour on pupils' wellbeing.

Preventing and Tackling Bullying	Guidance	'Bullying is behaviour by an individual or group, repeated over time, that intentionally hurts another individual or group either physically or emotionally. Bullying can take many forms (for instance, cyberbullying via text messages, social media or gaming, which can include the use of images and video) and is often motivated by prejudice against particular groups, for example on grounds of race, religion, gender, sexual orientation, special educational needs or disabilities, or because a child is adopted, in care or has caring responsibilities. It might be motivated by actual differences between children, or perceived differences.'	The Preventing and Tackling Bullying Guidance sets out: • a definition of bullying • schools' legal duties for addressing bullying on and off school grounds • different types of bullying • how to deal with bullying through prevention and intervention • support for staff who are bullied • further sources of information on LGBT bullying.
Keeping Children Safe in Education	Statutory guidance	'Safeguarding and promoting the welfare of children is *everyone's* responsibility. *Everyone* who comes into contact with children and their families has a role to play. In order to fulfil this responsibility effectively all practitioners should make sure their approach is child-centred. This means that they should consider, at all times, what is in the *best interests* of the child.'	Keeping Children Safe in Education details how schools and colleges in England must safeguard and promote the welfare of children when carrying out their duties. The guidance sets out: • a child-centred and coordinated approach to safeguarding • the role of school and college staff • what school and college staff need to know regarding child protection, behaviour and safeguarding • what school and college staff should look out for regarding child protection, behaviour and safeguarding • what school and college staff should do if they have concerns about a child • indicators of abuse and neglect • further information on peer on peer abuse, sexual harassment and risks for LGBT children, disabled children and those living with special educational needs.

Cont.

DOCUMENT	TYPE	QUOTE	SUMMARY OF RELEVANCE
Relationships and Sex Education Guidance	Statutory guidance	'To embrace the challenges of creating a happy and successful adult life, pupils need knowledge that will enable them to make informed decisions about their wellbeing, health and relationships and to build their self-efficacy…schools are free to determine how they address LGBT specific content, but the Department recommends that it is integral throughout the programmes of study.'	The Relationships and Sex Education Guidance details a range of requirements for statutory RSE, including: • developing a policy that complies with the Equality Act 2010 and inclusive of LGBT pupils, disabled pupils and those with special educational needs • working with parents, carers and the wider community • teaching strategies for relationships and sex education • safeguarding, reports of abuse and confidentiality.
Relationships and Sexuality Education (Wales)	Statutory guidance	'Explores the interconnected ways in which a wide and diverse range of social, cultural, technological and biological influences affect the ability to form and maintain positive relationships.'	The Relationships and Sexuality Education Guidance provides teachers and school staff with practical support to build high-quality provision of Relationships and Sexuality Education as part of a 'whole-school approach'. The curriculum must be: • inclusive • holistic • relevant, engaging and co-produced • creatively designed • empowering and transformative • protective and preventative.

Section 4: Who do I need to involve?

Utilising the skills of a motivated member of staff who is eager to drive the work forward, share their skills and champion lesbian, gay and bisexual inclusion is key to challenging homophobic and biphobic bullying. Appointing a member of staff to take ownership can inspire innovation and ensure the work is embedded across the school. It is however, vital that this person is supported by the senior leadership team to make connections with and engage wider stakeholders, including governors, parents, teaching staff and pupils. Everyone in the school has a role to play in affirming LGB equality and change-makers can be found everywhere from the classroom, Reception, the dining hall and the playground, to the school gates.

Governing body

School governors set the vision, ethos and strategic direction of the school and have a legal duty to ensure it meets its statutory safeguarding responsibilities. It is crucial that they are involved in work to challenge and prevent homophobic and biphobic bullying. They could be engaged by:

- appointing a named governor to support the school's work on LGB inclusion and maintain an overview of progress achieved

- briefing all the governors on the school's work on LGB inclusion

- ensuring that relevant policy changes are communicated to and ratified by the governors

- inviting governors to extend their knowledge by attending in-service training or external training days addressing homophobic and biphobic bullying

- involving the governors in pupil and parental engagement on the topic such as inputting into assemblies, attending parents' evenings or contributing to school newsletters.

Teaching and pastoral staff

Teaching and pastoral staff are on the frontline when it comes to addressing homophobic and biphobic bullying and vital to ensuring that policies are animated and acted on. Drawing on the skills and expertise of your colleagues can lead to a range of impactful and inventive initiatives. Here are three key steps to engaging your teaching and pastoral staff:

1 ESTABLISH A DIALOGUE

Taking the time to talk to the teaching and pastoral staff at your school can help provide a holistic view of its culture as well as establish investment in the work.

2 PROVIDE STAFF TRAINING

Empowering teaching and pastoral staff through training should be a priority for any school committed to preventing homophobic and biphobic bullying. Schools who achieve the most create multiple opportunities for their staff to develop the confidence, enthusiasm and knowledge to embed an LGB inclusive approach in their practice.

INVESTIGATE: Send key members of staff on external training to delve deeper into the specific areas in which you want to improve such as diversifying curriculum content or making materials inclusive of disabled pupils and those with special educational needs. Invite these staff members to cascade their learning at the next in-service training day, departmental meeting or twilight training session.

INTEGRATE: Dedicate an in-service training day to LGB inclusion to ensure that all school staff understand the school's policy on homophobic and biphobic bullying and how it applies to their area of practice.

INVIGORATE: Revisit the topic at regular intervals through online e-learning, twilight training or team meetings to ensure that progress is reviewed and knowledge stays fresh. For example, you may want to update staff on key terminology, inform them of significant legislative changes or share the outcomes of a particular piece of work.

3 FACILITATE RESOURCE AND SKILL SHARING

Scheduling opportunities for resource and skill sharing is a great way to celebrate and monitor the progress made by staff. This can occur online by maintaining a dedicated resource section on your staff portal and sending out email updates about available materials. It can also form part of regular departmental or pastoral meetings by establishing LGB inclusion as a standing agenda item.

Pupils

Children and young people have a right to be heard on the issues that matter to them and affect their lives (Article 12, United Nations Convention on the Rights of the Child). Pupils at your school will bring their own understanding of relationships and sexuality to school. Recognising and responding to their existing knowledge and experience is crucial to addressing homophobic and biphobic bullying cultures effectively as well as fostering respectful relationships between pupils. Utilising a range of engagement strategies can ensure that this work is relevant and responsive to your pupils needs. Below are some of the opportunities you can capitalise upon to work with pupils on LGB inclusion.

- Co-produced and cross-curricular relationships education: Develop your relationships education curriculum with pupils to ensure it is relevant to their emerging needs and embed these learning opportunities across all curricular subjects.

- Extra-curricular clubs: Working with extra-curricular groups such as your pupil parliament, student council, anti-bullying advisory groups and LGB societies can enrich efforts to address prejudice-based bullying cultures. These groups can help you review your anti-bullying policy, audit the curriculum and survey pupil views on how well the school affirms LGB equality.

- Awareness-raising dates: Capitalising upon awareness-raising days such as LGBT History Month, Pride or International Day Against Homophobia and Transphobia can link your work to local, national and global campaigns.

- School environment: Supporting pupils to contribute to a school display, poster campaign or library book collection addressing how the school values all families, cultures and relationships can be an excellent way to foster creativity and collaboration.

Parents and carers

Creating opportunities to work with parents and carers is crucial to affirming a whole-school approach to LGB inclusion. Enabling them to become familiar with curriculum materials, anti-bullying policies and school activities on LGB inclusion has the potential to enhance provision and foster cohesion between school and family messages about the topic.

Section 5: Where do I start?

Every school has different needs and requirements. Any process of change to your school's work on homophobic and biphobic bullying should be responsive to and led by your school community. Before deciding on your first or next step, it is useful to take stock of your current practice around fostering a safe and inclusive school environment.

Self-assessment and action planning

Does your pastoral team run excellent support services for LGB pupils but little of the curriculum content addresses their needs? Do you have a robust anti-bullying policy but struggle to keep track of prejudice-based incidents when they do occur? Perhaps your school excels at celebrating LGB equality but wants to refresh and diversify its approach?

The following steps provide a simple, interactive way to review current practice, identify priority areas for development and set goals for future work. They allow you to assess key areas of a whole-school approach including school leadership and policies, prevention work, staff training and responsiveness as well as pupil and parental engagement. These key first steps will help you make the most of your self-assessment and action planning.

STEP 1: ENLIST SUPPORT

It is vital that a member of the board of governors and senior leadership team is engaged in the process but you may also invite key pastoral staff and departmental heads to contribute too. Share your findings with other school leaders and governors to ensure they are briefed on the identified areas for improvement.

STEP 2: ENGAGE THE WIDER SCHOOL COMMUNITY

Does the wider school community share your priorities? Interview pupils and staff or conduct a brief survey to establish existing strengths, areas for improvement and where they feel resources need to be directed. Consult pupils and staff on what matters to them by conducting an LGB inclusive environment walk. Find out what other schools have been doing and whether there are any local organisations who can help you.

A whole-school approach to action planning

LGB inclusive environment walk

Invite adult volunteers from across the school community (e.g. governor, teacher, parent, support staff) to come together with pupil volunteers (e.g. school council, anti-bullying group, LGB society) and participate in an environment walk. Ask the team to look out for and take note of all the ways in which LGB inclusive school cultures are promoted around the school – for example, posters on display, books in the library, school signage, extra-curricular groups. Once the environment walk is complete, encourage the team to write a short report collaboratively of how well the school is doing, what needs to improve and how they will enact change in their role at the school.

STEP 3: PLAN AHEAD

- Identify what is achievable over the next month, the next term and the next academic year.

- Ensure that deadlines are set for key actions to be completed and someone is appointed to check in on progress.

- Remember to celebrate your achievements big and small and let the wider school community know how you are working to affirm a more LGB inclusive school culture.

Section 6: What's available to help me do this?
Inspiring Equality in Education School Resource

Policy and practice guidance covering what the law says, teaching about LGBT identities and relationships, handling disclosures, staff training and development, improving anti-bullying policies and one-to-one support for LGBT young people. Seven primary school targeted lesson plans covering celebrating difference, families, relationships, gender awareness and LGBT people in history. Nine secondary school targeted lesson plans on prejudice-based language or bullying, lesbian, gay, bisexual and trans lives, social media, prejudice and gender.

www.each.education/resources

Reach Teaching Resource

A resource for those working with young people to explore the vital issues of homophobia, sexism and cyberbullying. The resource is relevant for Years 7 to 13 (Key Stages 3, 4 and 5, ages 11–18) and includes lesson plans, group activity prompts, information about

National Curriculum links, awareness-raising posters and a DVD containing 13 short films.

www.each.education/resources

Anti-Homophobic Bullying Posters and Sexual Orientation Glossary

'She's gay and we're cool with that', 'He's gay and we're cool with that' and the Sexual Orientation/Gender Identity Glossary are three discrete posters all available from EACH's website.

www.each.education/resources

Educational Action Challenging Homophobia

- EACH delivers CPD accredited speaker led training and consultancy to help national and regional agencies (e.g. Health, Criminal Justice System, Social Services) better understand legislation regarding gender identity or sexual orientation matters to effect change at strategic and practical levels.
- Assists employers to develop best practice in supporting lesbian, gay, bisexual or trans employees and voluntary workers.
- Inspires schools, academies, colleges and universities to implement policy and procedural change concerning sexual orientation and gender identity issues through Department for Education and PSHE Association endorsed resources, training and consultancy: working with pupils, students, staff and governors.
- Delivers a national freephone helpline for young people to secure support following homophobic, biphobic or transphobic bullying.
- Integrates 30+ years' professional experience to inform books, Government commissioned national guidance and training including 'Safe to Learn' (DCSF), 'Inspiring Equality in Education' and 'Learn Equality Live Equal' (DfE), the 'Reach

Teaching Resource' (National Lottery), the Jessica Kingsley Publishers book, *That's So Gay! Challenging Homophobic Bullying* and Wales's statutory Schools' Anti-Bullying Guidance 'Rights, Respect, Equality' for its Government.

www.each.education/resources

Rights, Respect, Equality: Guidance for Schools

Statutory guidance forming part of a series of documents providing information for all involved in preventing and challenging bullying in Welsh schools. Each document in the suite gives advice for a key audience.

www.gov.wales/anti-bullying-guidance

AGENDA: A Young People's Guide to Making Positive Relationships Matter

AGENDA is a free online toolkit developed with young people, for young people. It supports them in how they can safely and creatively challenge gender inequalities and oppressive gender norms, both of which are the root cause and consequence of violence against girls and women, homophobia and transphobia. AGENDA has equality, diversity, children's rights and social justice at its heart and supports young people's rights to speak out and engage as active citizens on issues that matter to them. It is available in English and Welsh.

www.agenda.wales

Short, medium and long-term guide to challenging homophobic and biphobic bullying

TABLE A4.2: SHORT, MEDIUM AND LONG-TERM GUIDE

	SHORT-TERM ACTIONS	MEDIUM-TERM ACTIONS	LONG-TERM ACTIONS
LEADERSHIP, MANAGEMENT AND MANAGING CHANGE	Use a senior leadership team (SLT) meeting to appraise the school's current position on LGB matters. Pinpoints include how well the school believes it is dealing with homophobic and biphobic bullying. Ensure that each member of the SLT has read and digested the Equality Act 2010. Add or prioritise (as relevant) LGB inclusion on the school development plan.	Appoint a staff champion and deputies (in case the champion leaves or changes role) who will lead on this area: reviewing policy, supporting pupils and working towards a more inclusive community. EXAMPLE: Sir Bernard Lovell School has a daily meeting of SLT teachers, safeguarding and pastoral leads plus representation from the special educational needs team to discuss intersecting issues affecting individual pupils which have arisen during the day.	Set up a staff working group which collates and shares resources on inclusion and diversity with colleagues. Encourage staff to share lessons learned and 'make ordinary' conversations regarding gender identity and sexuality. Make staff visible to colleagues and pupils for example through use of badges, EACH's Safe Space stickers, rainbow lanyards or signs on classroom doors. Involve and train school governors on work to do with homophobic and biphobic bullying and lesbian, gay and bisexual inclusion. Ensure the head/SLT has provided a clear commitment to prevent and challenge HBT bullying via a whole-school approach to reach pupils, parents and staff. EXAMPLE: Make use of communicating through letters home to parents/carers, within staff induction/in-service training days, through statements on website and within your school's anti-bullying policy.
POLICY DEVELOPMENT	Check the school's anti bullying policy and include homophobic and biphobic bullying for review, update and revision. Ensure that all relevant policies reference the Equality Act. Ensure that policy includes information about how to report incidents to a member of staff.	Ensure your school's policy does not solely reference homophobic and biphobic bullying and the Equality Act but includes an explicit statement of commitment (as well as detail) on how the school monitors and plans to address the issue. Share ongoing policy development with parents, carers and governors.	Include pupils in the review and writing of policy so their investment is increased, they have a tangible stake in the process and its ongoing outcomes.

CURRICULUM, PLANNING AND RESOURCE	Review the PSHE curriculum for representation of LGB issues. Direct staff to resources online which might add to their awareness enhance their teaching practice.	Establish a curriculum audit with your school's pupils, identifying areas across subjects which can increase positive visibility of LGB people and history. Highlight key resources and books in library displays and regularly signpost pupils to these materials. EXAMPLE: Bristol Brunel Academy set up a dedicated area in the library for reading material aimed at LGB pupils or written by LGB authors.	Embed LGB representation across the curriculum and set up ways in which pupils can regularly feed back on areas for improvement and those working well or reflecting improvement. Run events such as workshops, invite guest speakers or creative sessions exploring different families and sexuality. EXAMPLE: Almondsbury Primary School's Pupil Parliament designed a poster illustrating the different types of bullying for a lower junior/infant audience. Ensure that there are resources and books readily available for pupils on gender identity and sexuality.
TEACHING AND LEARNING	Use a staff meeting to debate the value or otherwise of a 'zero-tolerance approach' to bullying in general and homophobic and biphobic bullying specifically. What position should one's school adopt? Capitalise upon teachable moments which raise awareness among pupils of the effect of homophobic language around the school.	Increase teacher training, supporting staff to develop lesson plans and vocabulary to use about the curriculum and around the school. Ensure cross-departmental knowledge of inclusive language, signs and symbols.	Empower pupils to be vocal and ensure zero tolerance. Support pupils to lead classes explaining HBT bullying; develop resources or host events celebrating LGB legislative change and its positive impacts on society. Regularly review teaching and learning for LGBT inclusion. EXAMPLE: Two Year 11 (ages 15–16) pupils delivered an assembly to their peers exploring the terminology to explain sexual orientation and encourage its appropriate and respectful use.
SCHOOL CULTURE AND ENVIRONMENT	Task relevant staff with auditing the environment – toilets, changing rooms, corridors, playgrounds and other communal areas – to assess safe and unsafe spaces around the school. EXAMPLE: Pupil engagement sessions with pupils highlighted 'unsafe' spaces they avoided hitherto unknown to the staff.	Raise awareness of the school's inclusive ethos and policy with visual displays and events for example LGBT+ History Month, Anti-Bullying Week, World AIDS Day. Ensure that diverse families and a variety of LGB role models are visible in multiple places around the school. EXAMPLE: Cotham School (Bristol) produced a corridor wall display as part of Pride awareness and an exploration of LGB authors.	Support LGB pupils to become leaders within the pupil population and lead on making LGB people an integral part of the curriculum. Regularly celebrate LGB equality. Draw the link between homophobic and biphobic bullying and adult hate crime and its consequences. Ensure that the school has a shared definition of what bullying is, that this is stated in policy and discussed among all staff and pupils.

Cont.

	SHORT-TERM ACTIONS	MEDIUM-TERM ACTIONS	LONG-TERM ACTIONS
GIVING PUPILS A VOICE	Task relevant members of staff to assess whether there are roles within pupil groups which focus on equality matters. Create simple feedback mechanisms for pupils to report incidents. EXAMPLE: Yeo Moor Primary School has various mechanisms by which pupils can disclose any bullying or other pastoral concerns such as a dedicated non-teaching pastoral member of staff and pupil engagement sessions with the headteacher.	Support pupils to establish a specific LGB support group or pupil equality group. Encourage LGB pupils to take positions of leadership and empower them to put their needs on the agenda. Support pupils to develop materials such as definition dictionaries, to be shared with staff and pupils. Provide regular drop-in sessions for pupils to come and discuss identity and inclusion with staff. Review how bullying is recorded and how data is analysed. EXAMPLE: Churchill Academy & Sixth Form has a thriving LGBT+ group – 'Libra' – meeting weekly.	Integrate pupil representatives within school decision-making. Regularly hear from Pupil Council/ house captains about pupil issues and encourage pupils to advise on changes to school policy. Establish pupils as partners in confronting matters concerning equality. Ensure that bullying is recorded by type that includes homophobic, biphobic or transphobic and sexist bullying and that data is regularly analysed, reported on and acted on. EXAMPLE: Almondsbury Primary School in South Gloucestershire has a Pupil Parliament which regularly appraises suggestions from infant and junior pupils as to how to make the school ever more inclusive, friendly and safe. It meets at least termly with an agenda of items to discuss and rewrote its school's anti-bullying policy in a poster format for pupil accessibility.
PROVISION OF PUPIL SUPPORT SERVICES	Task relevant staff to collate information about external support and resources accessible by your school's pupils. Ensure that this information is widely shared and accessible so pupils know where to go for support.	Integrate signposting to external services into the curriculum, using assemblies and PSHE as an opportunity to talk specifically about pupil support services. Share this information with parents and carers. EXAMPLE: Many schools use EACH's Safe Space stickers to assure or reassure pupils that a listening ear or signposting is available from the member of staff displaying these.	Establish in-school pastoral support and ensure it is integrated into the central running of the school. Regularly inform pupils that there is at least one member of staff with whom they can discuss anything to do with different families or sexuality. EXAMPLE: Yeo Moor Primary has a designated non-teaching member of staff with responsibility for pastoral care to whom children can go with any concerns.

STAFF PROFESSIONAL NEEDS, DEVELOPMENT AND WELFARE	Brief staff on LGB inclusion and embed LGB issues into continuing professional development. Outline plans for the school and invite participation, cooperation and feedback.	Train all staff specifically on encouraging LGB inclusion, embedding LGB representation into the curriculum and supporting LGB pupils to become empowered individuals. Embed LGB inclusion into safeguarding training.	Support pupils and pastoral staff to train teaching staff, building a team of 'experts' on LGB issues. Check in regularly with staff around their confidence in this area. Create a supportive atmosphere for staff to question and improve their understanding of LGB issues and language. Hold regular briefings and de-briefings to check in with staff on their delivery in this area. Make use of e-learning.
PARTNERSHIPS WITH PARENTS, CARERS AND LOCAL COMMUNITIES	Task relevant members of staff to assess whether parents have access to resources such as support information and designated members of staff to approach when matters arise. What information in newsletters, email bulletins, at parents' evenings and visible at other events attended by parents is currently available? Task a member of staff to assess this.	Regularly raise awareness with parents as to the school's activity on LGB inclusion. Host parental information sessions, networking opportunities, parent forums and so on. EXAMPLE: Bristol Brunel Academy has developed a 'Pride Pledge' with its pupils which has provided an ideal way to start looking at how to work with parents.	Run events in the community encouraging dialogue between community members, parents, pupils and teachers, for example parent forums and open mornings. Become a leading figure in the community for supporting marginalised pupils and challenging misconceptions.

(Contains public sector information acknowledging the Open Government Licence. Adapted from the National Children's Bureau and Educational Action Challenging Homophobia *Learn Equality Live Equal* programme (2018).)

Useful Organisations

ALBERT KENNEDY TRUST (AKT)

Supports LGBT 16–25-year-olds who are made homeless or are living in a hostile environment.

www.akt.org.uk

ANTI-BULLYING ALLIANCE

A coalition of organisations and individuals working together to stop bullying and create safe environments in which children and young people can live, grow, play and learn.

www.anti-bullyingalliance.org.uk

CHILDLINE

A private and confidential counselling service for children and young people up to the age of 19.

www.childline.org.uk

CHILD EXPLOITATION AND ONLINE PROTECTION CENTRE (CEOP)

Works with child protection partners across the UK and overseas to identify the main threats to children and coordinates activity against these threats to bring offenders to account.

www.ceop.police.uk

EDUCATIONAL ACTION CHALLENGING HOMOPHOBIA (EACH)

Since 2003, EACH has been the nation's provider of a dedicated Helpline giving young people up to 18 years old the opportunity to report and secure help further to homophobic, biphobic or transphobic bullying. It is a multiple award-winning charity delivering training and consultancy to education, children and young people's services, the criminal justice, Ministry of Defence and various statutory, voluntary and private sector organisations. EACH strives to increase understanding of sexual orientation, gender identity and online safety while helping agencies respond to and challenge homophobic, transphobic or cyber harassment in a variety of settings.

www.each.education

GALOP
LGBT+ anti-violence charity.

www.galop.org.uk

GENDER IDENTITY RESEARCH AND EDUCATION SOCIETY
Provides information for transgender people, their families and the professionals who care for them.

www.gires.org.uk

GENDERED INTELLIGENCE
A community interest company that looks to engage people in debates about gender. It works predominantly within young people's settings and has educative aims.

http://genderedintelligence.co.uk

HELPLINE – LGBT IRELAND
Supports, educates and connects people to enhance LGBT lives.

https://lgbt.ie

KIDSCAPE
A bullying prevention charity in England and Wales that provides practical support for children, families and schools.

www.kidscape.org.uk

LGBT YOUTH SCOTLAND

Provides quality youth work to LGBT young people and works in partnership for LGBTI equality and human rights.

www.lgbtyouth.org.uk

LGBT FOUNDATION

A national charity delivering advice, support and information services to lesbian, gay, bisexual and transgender people in the Greater Manchester area.

https://lgbt.foundation

LGBT NORTHERN IRELAND

A website to provide information to lesbian, gay, bisexual and transgender people and their families in Northern Ireland.

http://lgbtni.org

SWITCHBOARD

The @switchboard LGBT helpline provides an information, support and referral service for lesbians, gay men and bisexual and trans people – and anyone considering issues around their sexuality or gender identity. Open 10am–10pm every day on 0300 330 0630.

https://switchboard.lgbt

No responsibility can be taken for use made of any information provided by the above organisations, whose inclusion here is not an endorsement.

References

Aiden, H., Marston, K. and Perry, T. (2013) *Homophobic Bullying: How Well Do We Understand the Problem?* Bristol: EACH.

Ashenden, A. and Parsons, V. (2019) '15 rights LGBT people in the UK still don't have.' *Pink News*, 13/06/2019.

Askew, S. and Ross, C. (1988) *Boys Don't Cry: Boys and Sexism in Education.* Maidenhead: Open University Press.

BBC (2019) 'LGBT bullying in schools is more common than other kinds.' *BBC Newsround*, 04/07/2019.

Booth, R. (2019) 'Acceptance of gay sex in decline in UK for first time since AIDS crisis.' *The Guardian*, 11/07/2019.

Bowcott, O. (2017) 'UK issues posthumous pardon for thousands of gay men.' *The Guardian*, 31/01/2017.

Carr, A. (2014) 'Alan Carr: "The most homophobia I get is from gays".' *Pink News*, 16/04/2014.

Channel 4 (2019) Complaints Welcome. Available at: www.youtube.com/watch?v=h1xxC_Rr__U, accessed on 22/04/2020.

Charlesworth, J. (2004) *Out of the Shadow: Guidance to Bristol Schools on the Repeal of Section 28.* Bristol: Bristol City Council.

ChildLine Information Service (2019) personal communication, 24/10/2019.

Church of England Archbishops' Council Education Division (2014) *Valuing All God's Children: Guidance for Church of England Schools on Challenging Homophobic, Biphobic and Transphobic Bullying.* London: Church of England Archbishops' Council.

Department for Children, Schools and Families (2007) 'Homophobic bullying.' In *Safe to Learn: Embedding Anti-Bullying Work in Schools.* London: Department for Children, Schools and Families.

Department for Education (2013) *Teacher's Standards: Guidance for School Leaders, School Staff and Governing Bodies.* London: Department for Education.

Department for Education (2016) *Behaviour and Discipline in Schools: Advice for Headteachers and School Staff.* London: Department for Education.

Department for Education (2017a) *Exclusions from Maintained Schools, Academies and Pupil Referral Units in England: Statutory Guidance for Those with Legal Responsibilities in Relation to Exclusion.* London: Department for Education.

Department for Education (2017b) *FOI Release: Maintained Faith Schools.* London: Department for Education.

Department for Education (2017c) *Preventing and Tackling Bullying.* London: Department for Education.

Department for Education (2018) *Mental Health and Behaviour in Schools*. London: Department for Education.

Department for Education (2019a) *Statutory Guidance on Relationships Education, Relationships and Sex Education (RSE) and Health Education*. London: Department for Education.

Department for Education (2019b) *Guidance on Primary School Disruption over LGBT Teaching/Relationships Education*. London: Department for Education.

DitchTheLabel (2018) The Annual Bullying Survey 2018. Available at www.ditchthelabel. org/research-papers/the-annual-bullying-survey-2018, accessed on 05/03/2020.

Duffy, N. (2016) 'Lloyds bank features same-sex proposal in new TV ad.' *Pink News*, 14/02/2016.

EACH (2014) *Reach Teaching Resource: A Practical Toolkit for Challenging Homophobic, Sexist and Cyberbullying*. Bristol: EACH.

EACH (2016) *Inspiring Equality in Education: School Resource*. Bristol: EACH.

EACH (2018) *Learn Equality Live Equal*. Bristol: EACH [contains public sector information licensed under the Open Government Licence].

East Sussex and Brighton & Hove PSHE Advisory Team (2002) *The Sexuality Project: A Resource and Guidance Pack*. Brighton and Hove: PSHE Advisory Team.

Glasser, W. (1975) *Reality Therapy: A New Approach to Psychiatry*. London: Harper Collins.

Goddard, A. and Patterson, L. (2000) *Language and Gender*. London: Routledge.

Government Equalities Office (2011) Equality Act 2010: Public Sector Equality Duty. What Do I Need to Know? Available at https://assets.publishing.service.gov.uk/ government/uploads/system/uploads/attachment_data/file/85041/equality-duty. pdf, accessed on 22/04/2020.

Hobby, R. (2019) 'Teaching children about LBGT issues is not brainwashing – it equips them for life.' *The Guardian*, 09/06/2019.

Johnston, N. (2019) 'We refuse to be silenced about LGBT lessons, say Birmingham protest parents.' *The Times*, 04/06/2019.

Katz, A. (2013) *The Suffolk Cybersurvey*. London: Youthworks Consulting.

London Borough of Wandsworth Safeguarding Children Board (2012) *Anti-Bullying Strategy*. London: Corporate Communications Unit.

Lyons, I. (2019) 'Judge bans anti-LGBT protesters gathering outside primary school gates.' *The Telegraph*, 26/11/2019.

Marcus, L. (2019) 'Clever Dick: Dick Emery's Comic Creations.' *Television Heaven*, 27/11/2019.

Marsh, S., Mohdin, A. and McIntyre, N. (2019) 'Homophobic and transphobic hate crimes surge in England and Wales.' *The Guardian*, 14/06/2019.

Maslow, A.H. (1943) 'A theory of human motivation.' *Psychological Review*, 50: 370–396.

McCormick, J. (2016) 'Sainsbury's Christmas ad casually features a same-sex couple for a second year in a row.' *Pink News*, 14/11/2019.

METRO Youth Chances (2016) *Youth Chances: Integrated Report*. London: METRO.

Monk, D. (2011) 'Challenging homophobic bullying in schools: The politics of progress.' *International Journal of Law in Context*, 7 (2): 181–207.

Nansel, T.R., Overpeck, M., Pilla, R.S., Ruan, W.J., Simons-Morton, B. and Scheidt, P. (2001) 'Bullying behaviors among US youth: Prevalence and association with psychosocial adjustment.' *The Journal of the American Medical Association*, 285, 2094–2100.

Nunn, G. (2011) 'A challenge to the Guardian: It's time to drop the word "homosexual".' *The Guardian*, 18/11/2019.

Office for National Statistics (2019) *Religion in England and Wales*. London: Office for National Statistics.

Ofsted (2012) *No Place for Bullying: How Schools Create a Positive Culture and Prevent and Tackle Bullying*. Manchester: Ofsted.

Ofsted (2013) *Religious Education: Realising the Potential*. Manchester: Ofsted.

Ofsted (2014a) *Exploring the School's Actions to Prevent Homophobic Bullying*. Manchester: Ofsted.

Ofsted (2014b) *Inspecting E-safety in School*. Manchester: Ofsted.

Ofsted (2019) *The Education Inspection Framework*. Manchester: Ofsted.

Perry, K. (2008) 'Ur so gay.' Available at: www.youtube.com/watch?v=wy0wJutx7iU, accessed on 27/11/2019.

PETA (2014) 'Alan Carr: Be a Little Fairy for Animals!' Available at: www.peta.org.uk/blog/alan-carr-be-a-little-fairy-for-animals, accessed on 02/12/2019.

Pink News (2017) 'Gay couple causally star in Tesco's new Christmas advert.' *Pink News*, 10/11/2017.

Renold, E. (2013) *Boys and Girls Speak Out: A Qualitative Study of Children's Gender and Sexual Cultures*. Cardiff: Children's Commissioner for Wales.

Russell, B. (2013) 'School sex education policies accused of discriminating against homosexuality.' *Daily Express*, 20/08/2013.

Samsung (2019) 'The Future: What We Create Today Lets You Create the Future.' *Samsung Newsroom*, 02/02/2019.

Save the Children (2008) *Leave It Out: Developing Anti-Homophobic Bullying Practice in School*. Belfast: Save the Children.

Sex Education Forum (2019) *Young people's RSE poll 2019*. London: Sex Education Forum.

Sky News (2019) 'LGBT bullying more common than racist bullying in schools – poll.' *Sky News*, 04/07/2019.

Tolman, D. (2009) *Dilemmas of Desire: Teenage Girls Talk about Sexuality*. Cambridge, MA: Harvard University Press.

Trade Union Congress (2019) 'Sexual harassment of LGBT people in the workplace.' Available at www.tuc.org.uk, accessed on 05/03/2020.

Uber (2019) 'The Many Voices of Pride.' Available at: www.uber.com/en-GB/blog/the-many-voices-of-pride, accessed on 27/11/2019.

UK Government (1988) Local Government Act 1988. Available at www.legislation.gov.uk/ukpga/1988/9/section/28/enacted, accessed on 22/04/2020.

UK Government (2010) Equality Act 2010. Available at www.legislation.gov.uk/ukpga/2010/15/contents, accessed on 22/04/2020.

US Department of Health and Human Services (2011) *Working with Young People who Bully Others: Tips for Mental Health Professionals*. Washington: Department of Health and Human Services.

Webster, L. (2009) 'Lottery grant to Bristol gay teens' group "outrageous".' *Bristol Evening Post*, 27/08/2009.

Weiler, E. (2003) *Making School Safe for Sexual Minority Students*. Bethesda: National Association of School Psychologists.

Wells, K. (2019) NoHomophobes.com. Available at www.nohomophobes. com, accessed on 02/12/2019.

Welsh Government (2011) *Respecting Others: Homophobic Bullying Guidance Document*. Cardiff: Welsh Government.

Welsh Government (2019) *Rights, Respect, Equality: Guidance for Schools*. Cardiff: Welsh Government.

Youthworks (2017) The Suffolk Cybersurvey 2017. Available at www.suffolk.gov.uk/assets/community-and-safety/staying-safe-online/Suffolk-Cybersurvey-2017-final-report.pdf, accessed on 22/04/2020.

Youthworks (2019) personal communication, 20/11/2019.

Index

How to Transform Your School into an LGBT+ Friendly Place
A Practical Guide for Nursery, Primary and Secondary Teachers
Dr Elly Barnes MBE and Dr Anna Carlile

£14.99 | $19.95 | PB | 152PP |
ISBN 978 1 78592 349 4 | eISBN 978 1 78450 684 1

TEACH SECONDARY AWARDS FINALIST

Currently teachers don't receive the training or induction they need to make their school an LGBT+ inclusive environment. This can be seen by the fact that half of schools do not teach anything regarding LGBT+, and only 3% include LGBT+ content in two or more subjects. This book will help transform your school into a safe and inclusive place for all students.

Written with Educate & Celebrate!, an Ofsted and DfE recognised 'Best Practice Award Programme', this book gives teachers, governors and other staff the knowledge, strategies and confidence they need to implement a curriculum that is inclusive for all. Covering the changes to law, including the Equality Act 2010 that requires actively promoting acceptance, what language to use, case studies and much more, it is a must-have guide for all schools.

Dr Elly Barnes MBE is CEO and Founder of Educate & Celebrate and was voted #1 in *The Independent on Sunday*'s Rainbow List 2011.

Dr Anna Carlile is a Senior Lecturer in Inclusive Education at Goldsmiths, University of London, UK.

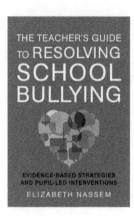

The Teacher's Guide to Resolving School Bullying
Evidence-Based Strategies and Pupil-Led Interventions
Elizabeth Nassem

£22.99 | $32.95 | PB | 232PP |
ISBN 978 1 78592 419 4 | eISBN 978 1 78450 785 5

Drawing on the author's cutting-edge research this practical book helps teachers better understand the causes of bullying, gives them confidence to resolve nuanced cases and provides them with the tools to develop pupil-led anti-bullying campaigns.

This book delves into the complex nature of bullying at school in a clear and approachable way. It helps school staff understand the student's views and experiences of bullying, and how power imbalances and systemic inequalities can contribute to bullying relationships between pupils. The author provides evidence-based interventions that suggest ways teachers can develop knowledge and skills to resolve incidents. Key to this is a new approach to pupil-led interventions which allows staff to harness pupil voices to develop effective anti-bullying strategies.

Included are resources and tools to help teachers set up these advisory groups and interventions, and train others to do the same. This is essential reading for teachers looking for a comprehensive and accessible guide to tackling bullying.

Dr Elizabeth Nassem is a consultant and researcher in school bullying. She is the founder of Bullied Voices which provides research-informed anti-bullying strategies in education establishments. Elizabeth specialises in designing, implementing and evaluating evidence-based pupil-led anti-bullying interventions in schools. Her work has frequently featured in the national media such as BBC Radio 5 Live and *The Telegraph*. She lives in West Yorkshire.

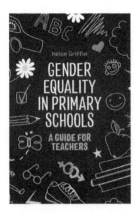

Gender Equality in Primary Schools
A Guide for Teachers
Helen Griffin

£14.99 | $22.95 | PB | 216PP |
ISBN 978 1 78592 340 1 | eISBN 978 1 78450 661 2

This hands-on guide supports primary teachers and other school staff in challenging gender stereotypes and sets out advice on how to implement gender equality and respect in the curriculum, and in all areas of school life.

An increase in the number of transgender children – and a recognition of gender reassignment as a protected characteristic under the 2010 Equality Act – means that all primary schools need to ensure they are safe environments respectful of all genders. This book draws on the 'Gender Respect Project', which identified the need to address gender stereotyping and gender-based violence with children and young people.

The book is full of lesson plans, case studies, clear guidance and recommended actions as well as further reading and resources. Extending beyond awareness of other genders, this book provides a framework for a gender equality approach in the classroom and empowers children to think critically about gender and to respect themselves and others.

Helen Griffin is Global Education and Philosophy for Children Advisor and Joint Coordinator of the Development Education Centre South Yorkshire, and was project lead on the 'Gender Respect Project'.